GW01185279

JULY

Minor Prophets: Part 1

IAN COFFEY

AUGUST

Ephesians

PETER HICKS

PLUS ...

Weekend reflections on the Psalms,
and the Big Picture by Philip Greenslade

CWR

MIX
Paper from
responsible sources
FSC® C015900
www.fsc.org

Ian Coffey

Ian Coffey is Vice Principal and Director of Leadership Training at Moorlands College on the south coast of England. An ordained Baptist minister, he has been involved in church leadership for over 30 years. He has authored 14 books and speaks at conferences and events in many countries. Ian is married to Ruth and they have four adult sons and two granddaughters. In both writing and speaking his passion is to explain and apply the message of the Bible in everyday language.

Peter Hicks

Peter Hicks has been engaged in ministry and preparing others for ministry for over 40 years. Born in Bristol, he has pastored churches in the Midlands and the London area, and served on the staff of London Bible College/ London School of Theology where he specialised in philosophy and pastoral theology. He has written a number of books on Christian living and issues such as the nature of truth and the problem of evil. He and his wife Gwen are currently involved in an outreach project in rural Wales.

Philip Greenslade

Having originally trained for the Baptist ministry, Philip has over 30 years' experience in Christian ministry. He has worked with CWR since 1991 in the areas of biblical studies, pastoral care and leadership. With his passion for teaching God's Word, he offers a refreshing and challenging perspective for all those who attend his courses. Close to Philip's heart are the long-running Bible Discovery Weekends. Course Director for CWR's recent postgraduate programme in Pastoral Leadership, Philip is currently leading a Pastoral Care course focused on Christian identity and vocation. He is the author of several books including *God's Story, Voice from the Hills* and *Ministering Angles*.

Copyright © CWR 2007, 2012

First published 2007 by CWR. This edition published 2012 by CWR, Waverley Abbey House, Waverley Lane, Farnham, Surrey GU9 8EP, England. CWR is a Registered Charity – Number 294387 and a Limited Company registered in England – Registration Number 1990308.

Unless otherwise indicated, all Scripture references are from the Holy Bible: New International Version (NIV), copyright © 2001, 2005 by Biblica. Used by permission of Biblica®. Other versions: ESV: The Holy Bible, English Standard Version, published by HarperCollins Publishers © 2001 by Crossway Bibles, a division of Good News Publishers. Used by permission. NLT: Holy Bible New Living Translation, © 1996. Used by permission of Tyndale House Publishers Inc. RSV: Revised Standard Version, © 1965, Division of Christian Education of the National Council of the Churches of Christ in the United States of America. *The Message*: Scripture taken from *The Message*. Copyright © 1993, 2002. Used by permission of NavPress Publishing Group. AV: *The Authorised Version*.

Concept development, editing, design and production by CWR

Cover image: sxc/Gabriel Quintão

Printed in England by Linney Print

Minor Prophets: Part 1
Ian Coffey

TUCKED AWAY at the back of the Old Testament lies a group of forgotten heroes. Men with strange-sounding names such as Nahum, Haggai, Zechariah and Obadiah have suffered from an overdose of neglect. They are not helped by Augustine labelling them as *The Minor Prophets*. He did this with reference to their size, as their books are short compared to those of the heavyweights – Isaiah, Jeremiah, Ezekiel and Daniel. But for some, the word 'minor' is misinterpreted as 'not all that important'.

However, the 12 prophets who fall into this category do have an important part to play in the unfolding story of the Bible. Prophets didn't simply predict the future. They addressed the *here and now issues* of their day. They had a dual task of forthtelling (speaking out about contemporary issues) and foretelling (bringing God's word about where history was heading). Their job proved a lonely assignment, and many of them suffered because of their obedience to God's call. They are included in the roll call of honour for heroes and heroines of faith that we find in Hebrews 11:32–38.

This month we shall consider six of them and notice how they:
- listened hard to God
- reflected deeply about their world
- shared God's message with courage.

And those are qualities we *all* need to develop as we grow as disciples of Christ.

How long?

WAITING IS irritating at the best of times; at the worst it is almost unendurable. Even more so where God's promises and presence are concerned.

This psalm is not the voice of cynical unbelief but of faith crying out in the darkness. So the psalmist questions God, not in airily academic detachment, but *out of a profound sense of God's absence.*

His fourfold 'how long?' launches an emotional dialogue with God which is characteristic of Old Testament faith, not least of the prophets (cf. Hab. 1:2; Zech. 1:12; cf. Isa. 6:11).

What is being expressed here is the dark side of faith – known in some measure at least to every genuine believer; namely, the sense of being forgotten by God, of God's face averted in seeming disfavour (v.1), of relentless mental turmoil and inner debate (v.2a), and of knowing a 'sadness that never goes away' as enemies seem more in control than God (v.2b).

The pain of God's hiddenness and delay forces urgent prayer (v.3): 'look' – notice me, Lord; 'answer' – respond to my plight; 'give light' – let me see the dawn of a new day.

Even though we now enjoy the richness of our new covenant experience, we may still feel the need to pray such prayers.

A psalm like this serves as a reality check on fantasy faith.

It offers a healthy dose of realism to an overheated faith that claims too much too soon from God.

It tells us to expect 'dark nights of the soul'; *not necessarily* to be interpreted as a sign that we have sinned. Rather, psalms like this may teach us that God trusts us to trust Him even when we don't feel He is near! Above all, such experiences and prayers alert us to the danger of trying to control God or deny Him the freedom of action which we fiercely demand for ourselves.

And, when all is said and done, all is not said or done!

No negative experience can finally undermine for us the reality of God's enduring covenant-love or erase the memory of His goodness (vv.5–6). *That* love we can trust to sustain us even in the dark.

Tough call

Hosea faced a tough call when God appointed him His spokesman to the rebellious northern kingdom of Israel, made up of the ten tribes that had broken away to form a separate kingdom. Within a few years an Assyrian invasion would end their plans and thousands would be led away to exile.

Hosea lived during the last days of this kingdom that saw six kings in the short space of 25 years. The call to serve Yahweh, the God of Israel, was very hard for Hosea, not simply because he had to bring bad news to his own countrymen. The toughest part of the call was that Hosea's own family life was to be a living illustration of his message.

Our reading explains just how difficult this was. Israel had been unfaithful to God – and Hosea was told to marry a woman who would cheat on him too (vv.2–3). It has been suggested that he married a prostitute, although others claim Gomer did not become adulterous until after their marriage. Some find the idea that God would call a person to this kind of marriage so shocking they claim it is a parable rather than a real account.

Hosea and Gomer had three children, whose names are a sermon in themselves: Jezreel (v.4), which means *God scatters*, Lo-Ruhamah (v.6), meaning *not loved*, and Lo-Ammi (v.9) – *not my people* – whose name suggests Hosea may not have been his father. These are hardly names happily married parents would give their children to carry for life, but they denote something very serious about the state of the nation. Hosea's sad marriage mirrored the breakdown in Israel's covenant with Yahweh. God's people had been an unfaithful partner.

Yet today's reading concludes on a note of hope and grace. It's a vision of the future for a reunited nation and a fresh start. It will be called the day of Jezreel – but the 'scattering' will be of seed for a bumper harvest (v.11).

Even the darkest clouds of judgment cannot totally eclipse God's grace.

Lusting for lovers

Hosea's troubled family life was not a private matter. He couldn't hide his wife's affairs, especially from his children. He even appealed to them to challenge her behaviour (v.2). His brokenness fuelled his passionate preaching: Israel was behaving like an adulterous woman lusting for lovers (v.7). As someone has commented, 'Hosea's grief became his gospel.'

Just as Gomer had run after other men, so Israel had turned to other gods. Baal (v.8), was a Canaanite god who, it was believed, controlled the weather and provided fertility for crops, animals and people. This was more than swapping denominations. Baal worship involved making offerings to idols and having sexual relations with so-called sacred prostitutes (both male and female). Such 'worship' was a symbolic ritual denoting the need for the land to be fertilised – but its destructive effects on the nation are not difficult to imagine.

This spiritual adultery meant that Israel mistakenly believed Baal provided the good harvests, so Yahweh decided to discipline the nation with failed crops and other hardships (vv.11–13). The idea of God disciplining His children was not new to Hosea (eg Psa. 81:10–16), and we should look at some of our own hardships in this light. Are my current financial problems being used by God to teach me to be more faithful in my giving? Is that situation at work part of God's discipline (or *discipling*) process to make me less arrogant and more trusting?

It is important we don't miss the stunning conclusion to this chapter (vv.14ff.). Despite the Israelites' disobedience and rejection of the Lord who had delivered them from Egypt, He has not rejected them for ever. The place known as the Valley of Trouble, where a tragic episode in the nation's history had occurred (see Josh. 7:24), would be made a doorway of hope (v.15). God's discipline has a positive purpose – to bring us closer to Himself. The new names for Hosea's children point to this (v.23). God's discipline is remedial – drawing us back to Himself.

Is He wooing you today? Then listen to His tender voice (v.14).

CWR
Ministry Events

Please pray for the team

DATE	EVENT	PLACE	PRESENTERS
4 Jul	Effective RE Teaching – Equipping the Non-specialist	Waverley Abbey House	Lorraine Abbott
5 Jul	Church Leaders' Forum	WAH	Andy Peck and Philip Greenslade
10 Jul	Mentoring Others	WAH	Peter Jackson
11 Jul	Small Group Leaders' Evening	WAH	Andy Peck with Lynette Brooks
14 Jul	Insight into Self-harm	WAH	Chris Ledger
14 Jul	Money Matters	WAH	Stephen and Rosalyn Derges
16–20 Jul	Woman to Woman Training Course	WAH	Lynn Penson and team
16–20 Jul	Seniors Summer Holiday	Pilgrim Hall	Derek Martin
21 Jul	Growing as They Grow	WAH	Rachel Causey
23–27 Jul	Refreshing Your View of the Bible	WAH	Philip Greenslade and team
4–11 Aug	Family Summer Holiday	Pilgrim Hall	Charles Earwickers
6–9 Aug	Developing an Integrative Christian Approach to Counselling	WAH	Mary Higginson
11 Aug	Handling the Pressure	WAH	Beverley Shepherd
13–17 Aug	Introduction to Biblical Care and Counselling	WAH	Angie Coombes, Richard Laws and team
18 Aug	Living Singly for God's Glory	WAH	Julia Morgan
20–24 Aug	BA Counselling Year 1 starts	WAH	Heather Churchill
20 Aug	Certificate of Christian Counselling starts	WAH	Irene Davies
28 Aug – 1 Sep	BA Counselling Year 2 starts	WAH	Heather Churchill

Join us on 9 September for an 'open house' with a cream tea, to celebrate 25 years at Waverley Abbey House. **For further information visit our website.**

For full details phone 01252 784719, international +44 (0)1252 784719 or see the CWR website for further information.

www.cwr.org.uk

Buy her back!

I cannot begin to imagine the humiliation Hosea must have felt as he made his way to the brothel to haggle over the price of his wife. Yet, despite her unfaithfulness, the Lord told him to show his love for her (3:1). Hosea had to pay for his wife to be released from a dreadful mess. The price of a slave was 30 shekels, but he could only muster half the price and made up the balance in produce (3:2). This was costly in every sense – but redemption always is.

Hosea imposes a cooling-off period during which they would live together, but not in a full relationship. Like an alcoholic being weaned off drink, Gomer needs to stay away from sex (3:3). And God reveals how this is a picture of what is about to happen to Israel – His unfaithful bride. A period of exile is coming when familiar things will be stripped away, and a new sense of respect for Yahweh will result (3:4–5). Hosea's act of grace and remedial discipline in his own marriage is a mirror image of what God will do with His wayward people. He doesn't want rid of them; He wants a change of attitude and behaviour.

Our reading spells out the nature of God's charge against His rebellious people (4:1). By deserting Him they have let their personal standards slide, and the whole land has suffered as a result (4:2–3). Those who were so-called men of God – priests and prophets – had failed to set an example in life and teaching (4:4–9). Family life was disintegrating, and, in the topsy-turvy world of double standards, men were engaging in extra-marital sex yet looking horrified when their children followed their dreadful example (4:13–14). God, however, will not intervene. They are drunk, stupid and unfaithful (4:10–12), believing a wooden statue governs their wellbeing. The Lord pronounces the judgment of futility: their desires for fruitfulness in field and family will end in frustration.

A spirit (or attitude) of prostitution (4:12), and endemic stubbornness (4:16), are God's diagnosis. The danger is that their fellow Israelites across the border in Judah may catch the disease too (4:15).

Mean what you say

The way to understand the book of Hosea is to spot how it is put together. Chapters 1 to 3 detail the painful and puzzling family life of Hosea and draw parallels with Israel's unfaithfulness. The remaining chapters are a collection of Hosea's messages, delivered over a period of years.

At the heart of today's reading lies a stunning statement (6:6): God is not as religious as we might think! The Israelites were caught up with the rituals of religion, but Yahweh wants loyal love and obedience more than anything else. The word 'mercy' is a key Bible word; in Hebrew it is *hesed*, which combines the ideas of loyalty and love. There is no direct equivalent in English, but David Pawson sums it up in a memorable phrase: it is a 'stay-with-it love'.

The repentance described (6:1–3) is not deep, nor is it real; it is a superficial response that betrays this attitude: 'We're in a jam – quick, let's ask God to forgive us.' This repentance is no more than a mist that vanishes with the rising sun. In the New Testament

Paul warns against that kind of worldly sorrow, which leads to spiritual death (2 Cor. 7:10). The Lord wants Israel to 'get real'.

Hosea refers to places and incidents that would have struck a chord with his audience, and we can only speculate about the details. But the thrust of his message is unambiguous: kings, priests and people have arrogantly turned from Yahweh in this act of spiritual adultery (5:1–5). Instead of being loyal to Him and seeking His will they have turned to the Assyrians for protection (5:13). They entered into costly peace agreements in the belief that this would safeguard their security. Yet the Assyrians were the very ones who would sack the land eventually. Yahweh Himself, would stand against them and would distance Himself until reality dawned and genuine heartfelt repentance was evident (5:14–15).

These are sobering words that challenge those things we put our trust in, highlight the danger of superficial repentance, and caution against a worship life built on ritual rather than reality. Let's mean what we say.

Sowing and reaping

A friend underwent a medical examination, and, as a result, he made some radical changes to his way of living. When I enquired what the doctor had told him, he gave a stark reply: 'Either you change your habits or you will die.'

Hosea's message has the same ring of painful honesty. First, there is a diagnosis. Israel had blatantly ignored God's law and had even come to consider the carefully recorded books of Moses as foreign (8:12). Ignoring God's Word was the first step on a slippery slope because one of the functions of Scripture is to keep us mindful of God and His ways (8:14).

The symptoms were obvious, and Hosea describes them: dishonesty, theft, political intrigue and drunkenness are all mentioned (7:1–5). Hosea speaks directly concerning the circumstances of his day. The people of Israel were seeking political alliances with surrounding nations, such as Assyria and Egypt, which was senseless (7:11). And, because they failed to seek God's help, they will fall (7:16).

In a vivid turn of phrase Hosea sums up the disease: Israel is like a half-baked cake burnt to a crisp on one side and a soggy uncooked mess on the other (7:8). These foreign alliances were robbing the nation of its strength, and the tragedy was compounded by ignorance that things had become so bad.

One sad episode in the nation's decline came shortly after the division of the 12 tribes. Jeroboam I was the first ruler of the northern kingdom, and he lived about 60 years before Hosea. In order to prop up his rebellious regime he had made two golden calves and declared them to be the gods who had rescued Israel from Egypt (1 Kings 12:25–30). With great courage, Hosea delivers God's verdict on this act of adultery (8:4–6). He goes right to the very heart of daily life in Israel and exposes those things that grieved Yahweh and blighted their covenant relationship with Him. His sermon is summed up in a word picture: sow the wind and you reap the whirlwind (8:7).

Choices have consequences. And what was true for Israel in the eighth century BC remains true for us in the twenty-first century AD.

Worship as **lifestyle**

THE ELEVEN answers given in this psalm to the original question it poses, reaffirm the integration of daily life and weekly worship.

It is a truism to say that biblical faith never separates the sacred and the secular. Of course, the Torah's laws of holiness distinguish well enough between what is clean and unclean, sacred and common (see Leviticus). But these careful distinctions only serve to show that everything is brought within the scope of the worshipping life.

This psalm echoes the prophetic critique of unworthy worship – worship that is divorced from godly work, worship on one day of the week which is contradicted by the unjust social practices of the other six days of the week (cf. Amos 5:21–24; 8:4–6).

The psalm also reflects typical priestly instructions for how worshippers may approach God in the sanctuary. As such, it reminds us that God has the right to determine when, where, how, and by whom He is worshipped. This is a healthy check on the modern assumption that worship springs from our feelings and can take any shape we choose to express them by. On the contrary, biblical worship is a covenantal response to the kind of covenantal obligations mentioned by the psalmist.

The psalm celebrates the paradoxical unapproachability of God's holiness and the accessibility of His grace. On the one hand, it warns us against hypocrisy and, on the other, guards us against casual approaches to God.

And if, as this psalm confirms, the goal of worship is to encounter God and to dwell again in His holy and gracious presence, which of us would want to miss that by careless living?

Better to walk the talk, to let our speech match our songs, to keep our promises even to our own disadvantage.

True worship is a lifestyle, the glorifying of God in everything we do – a consistent thread of truth throughout the Bible (cf. 1 Cor. 10:31). It is the well-integrated life that proves stable and unshakeable and that best honours God.

A twig on the water

There are times when it is costly to speak up for what is right. Hosea lived with the personal pain of his own marriage, but there is evidence from today's reading that he also faced public hostility for his forthright preaching. According to him, sin had such a destructive effect on the collective conscience that anyone with a word from God was considered mad (9:7–8). Yet he stayed true to his calling to be a faithful watchman. This is a timely reminder for us to stay on course and not be blown about by popular opinion.

Harvest was usually a time for celebration and thanksgiving, but sadly for Israel these times were about to end. Exile in Assyria beckoned and the party was about to become a funeral wake (9:1–4). The reference to returning to Egypt is poetic, not literal. Just as the nation had languished as slaves in Egypt so once again they would be prisoners in a foreign land. Yahweh – the God of the covenant – is about to reject them because of their persistent disobedience (9:17).

Thinking back to that period when God rescued them out of Egypt, Hosea paints a picture of the farmer finding fruit on the vine or fig tree. But soon the crop was ruined (9:10). Hosea knew his nation's history well – including the unsavoury parts. ('Baal Peor' refers to a dark incident recorded in Num. 25:1ff.)

Though Yahweh had shown limitless patience with these rebellious people, they had remained deaf and blind. Their idols would follow them into exile as plunder seized by the Assyrian army (10:5–6), Samaria, their capital, would fall, and their king along with it. Like a twig carried downstream in a river, the securities of king and capital would be swept away (10:7). In 722 BC – a few years after Hosea preached his challenging message – this prophecy was fulfilled.

Yet, within this prophecy of judgment there is a kernel of grace (10:12). The picture is of a plough cutting across hard ground, good seed being planted, showers falling and a bumper crop being harvested. It reminds us of the continual need of tender hearts to provide good soil (see Matt. 13:1–9).

Glimpsing God's heart

Chapter 11 is one of the greatest passages in the Bible – in it we glimpse God's heart. Here is no angry, vengeful God. Instead we find a portrait of a tender father teaching his little child to walk (11:3), and a caring farmer freeing an animal from the yoke and stooping to feed it (11:4). Such poetic language reminded Hosea's audience that, although God had delivered them from the slavery of Egypt (11:1), they had repaid Him with spiritual unfaithfulness.

Hosea's personal pain at his wife's many betrayals lies at the core of the heart-cry from God he so passionately declared (11:8). Hosea had wanted to give up on his relationship with Gomer – but his love for her was greater than his anger. His grief allowed him to glimpse the heart of God towards His covenant people. For all their unfaithfulness He could not totally blot them out as He did Admah and Zeboiim, the two towns destroyed with Sodom and Gomorrah (11:8; see Gen. 19:24–25; Deut. 29:23).

Here is a stunning revelation: God bears on His *own* heart the pain caused by His rebellious people. This truth points towards the cross of Christ, when God Himself would bear our sins.

Hosea's sermon is rich in Old Testament imagery as he declares the people are liars (11:12), as seen by their political double-dealing with two competing nations (12:1). They follow in the twisting ways of their forefather Jacob – yet even he sought God with tears and changed his ways (12:2–6). They are like a dodgy trader blinded by his wealth and pride (12:7–8), and judgment in the form of exile awaits them.

Some struggle to understand how God can love people and yet punish them for their sin. They feel there is a contradiction in God's character. That is why we need the whole sweep of Scripture to give us a complete picture. Hosea's insight shows us sin not only offends God's character, it also breaks His heart. Compare today's reading with Genesis 6:6 and ask God for grace to glimpse His heart. And, perhaps for some of us, grace to let Him use our own sense of rejection and loss to grant insight into His feelings towards a rebellious world.

Walking straight

Ephraim had been the largest tribe of Israel and had commanded respect – but all this had gone through idol worship and everything that was caught up with it. Verse 2 of chapter 13 is hard to translate, but the suggestion is that they had even sacrificed children. Hosea's voice drips with sarcasm at the notion that people kissed the idols made with their own hands. Their pride had made them forgetful of Yahweh's many kindnesses (13:6), and their desire to be like other nations by having a king had ended in disaster (13:10–11). Since several kings were murdered during this period, this struck a chord with Hosea's audience.

Once again, Hosea's vivid imagery brings home his point. Like a woman in labour who gives birth to a stillborn child so all the potential blessing for Israel will die (13:13).

Notice, however, that this solemn message is not without windows of hope. Hosea anticipates the rebirth of the nation (13:14), and Paul, the Christian leader, quotes this statement in the New Testament when he describes the final victory of Jesus over death (1 Cor. 15:55). God always wants to redeem rather than write off.

The final chapter of Hosea's collection of sermons could be subtitled 'Finding your way back to God', and it is worth thinking about its wise advice. Honest words are important (14:2), as well as a willingness to change our behaviour (14:3). We should cast ourselves on the mercy of God and trust Him to restore us (14:4). The picture of fruitful fields and flourishing trees is often used to describe the blessings of God. But remember, Israel had chased after other gods to achieve these things – and when they did so the harvests had failed. The principle is clear: live God's way if you want to enjoy God's blessings.

The final verse of Hosea's book may well have been added by another hand (14:9) – maybe by an editor working hard to preserve his valuable messages. It forms a timely postscript and reminds us to ask the question, 'What does the message of Hosea tell me about walking in God's way?' Wise and discerning people take note!

Getting behind the headlines

I have never seen a swarm of locusts but those who have tell a frightening story. Swarms can be several hundred square kilometres in size, with up to 80 million locusts per square kilometre. They can eat in a day what 40,000 people consume in a year. They strip every piece of living vegetation – even the bark of trees. Plagues of locusts have been documented from ancient times to the modern day. There were five widespread plagues in the last century, and the United Nations employs a full-time team called 'Locust Watch' to monitor potential plagues because of the huge economic implications of an attack.

Joel describes one such devastating locust plague in the opening verses of his book. He uses the word picture of an invading army (vv.6–7) that has totally ruined the trees and fields (v.4). It's not only the farmers and vine-growers who are affected; the whole nation suffers from the impact of this plague. Grain and wine offered in worship services have vanished, along with the harvest (v.9), and the joy of life has been stripped away like the leaves from the trees (v.12).

We know very little about Joel as a man, and there has been much debate as to when he lived. His book makes no reference to key events which would help us pinpoint where he fits in history. What is obvious is that he is referring to a serious locust plague that had severe economic consequences. And though we may not know when this happened, his listeners did!

But notice he is not simply an anxious news journalist reporting a national disaster. He looks behind the headlines and calls the nation to get their lives straight with God. He urges the spiritual leaders to fast and seek God with repentant hearts (vv.13–14), and he includes himself in this act of penitence (vv.19–20). It was C.S. Lewis who described pain as a megaphone God sometimes uses to rouse a deaf world. I am challenged today by Joel's example of looking behind the headlines. Jesus encouraged the people of His day to do just that and to discern God's voice (Luke 13:1–5). May we, too, be tuned in as we read today's news.

Alarm call

Joel called for an alarm to wake God's people (v.1). God's day had arrived in the form of a locust plague. When Joel paints a vivid picture of locusts acting like an invading army which destroys everything in its path (vv.1–11), he is probably writing about an event that had already happened. His sermon is an explanation of why it had occurred. And it's alarming: the Lord is at the head of this invading 'army' (v.11).

Imagine you were surveying your own ravaged fields and wondering if you could feed your family. As you pray, you discover the Lord is behind the plague, and your sense of loss becomes even greater. But Joel is only explaining what God had already revealed about the consequences of disobedience (see 2 Chron. 7:13–14). This is a call to God's people to turn back to Him and clean up their lives.

I am struck by the depth of the penitence that is called for. It's more than a hasty 'Sorry Lord'. It is a call to whole-hearted repentance that goes beyond torn clothes (a symbol of grief) to a torn heart (vv.12–13). That is deep.

But it's also broad. Everyone in the nation is included – young and old, leaders and priests. Even the happy couple on their wedding day are called to put their plans on hold (vv.15–17). It is a call to the whole community to gather and seek God's forgiveness.

Notice, though, two things that wrap this challenge in grace. First, there is the assurance of hope, forgiveness and a fresh start. There is the wonderful promise that the ravages of the locusts will be somehow miraculously repaid (v.25). (I wonder how many people have found a promise of a new beginning through reading this verse?) Then there is the promise that the gift of God's Spirit will be poured out in the last days (vv.28–32). Eight hundred years later Peter quoted this passage on the Day of Pentecost (Acts 2:14ff.). And another 2,000 years on we are reading it and marvelling at its relevance today. This reminds us that this is not Joel's word – but God's. What is He saying to me through it today?

Never **underestimate** God

TO A FANFARE the Judge enters. Court is in session; the whole earth is summoned to attend. The opening roll call of names is impressive: 'El' – chief of all gods (cf. v.14); 'Elohim' – God, the Creator and life-giver, and, above all, 'Yahweh' – Israel's covenant Lord.

And the One Creator God answers to them all as He arrives to convene the meeting, trailing fire and tempest in His wake – the classic signs of theophany reminiscent of Sinai (cf. Exod. 19). He comes to settle a covenant lawsuit with Israel (cf. the prophetic language of legal indictment; cf. Hos. 4:1–6; Micah 6:1–2).

The time has come to evaluate the relationship between Him and His people. He comes to summon them to *a covenant renewal* (v.5), with heaven and earth invoked as legal witnesses (cf. Deut. 4:26). They confirm that God has been faithful in keeping covenant with Israel (v.6), but what of His covenant partner?

The majestic opening alerts us to the main complaint God has against His people – that of *underestimating Him*.

The shift of scene from the fiery mountain, Sinai, to the humble hill, Zion (v.2) represents a significant advance of revelation, but one which can be easily misunderstood. At Sinai God kept His distance in unapproachable majesty; at Zion He draws near and invites us to dwell with Him.

This movement from Sinai to Zion is a movement 'downwards', a condescension of God from mystery to intimacy, from being wholly 'above' us to being also 'with us'. But we seriously misread this if we mistake God's condescension for a reduction in His majesty. If we dissolve the vital tension between His 'farness' and His 'nearness' then we presume on His grace, trade on His approachability, and create a user-friendly God.

He retains all His majesty and mightiness. He refuses to be underestimated. In this covenant lawsuit, He re-asserts His 'Godness' to His people (v.7).

Though secure in covenant relationship with Him, we dare not domesticate Him, trivialise Him, or reduce His glory.

The last word

From my balcony I can see the Alps – French, Swiss and Italian. Some mountains are quite close, some mid-range, and a number far-distant. Towering above them all stands the white mountain – Mont Blanc – the highest peak in Europe. Meditating on today's reading I can imagine how Joel may have viewed the panorama of God's purposes in history.

Some things were close to him. The ill-treatment of his people by their neighbouring nations would not go unchecked (v.4). He could see some events like mountains in the mid-range of his vision – his prophecy of the Day of Pentecost (2:28ff.). And he viewed some big peaks in the far-distance. I believe part of Joel's prophecy relates to the final judgment of God on all people. The Valley of Jehoshaphat (vv.1,12) means 'the place where the Lord judges'. It points to a specific time when God's blessings will flow to His obedient people, and His judgment will rest on those who chose to walk in their own way. Joel, in his vivid poetry, refers three times to the earth and heavens shaking (2:10, 30–31; 3:15–16). The inference is that these are climactic moments in history when God is doing something significant in a cosmic sense. Joel's prophetic picture of the blessings awaiting the Lord's people compares with the portrait painted in the last pages of the Bible (see Rev. 22:1–6).

Looking over Joel's shoulder at the horizon as he saw it, we realise we live closer to some of those peaks that looked far-distant in his day. History is moving towards the end God has already written. The night before writing this I shared a meal with friends, and we reviewed some recent world events that have left people shaken. 'Where is it all heading?' someone asked. Today's reading answers that question loudly and clearly. God will have the last word at the victory celebration of the Lord Jesus. At moments of fear, that truth brings comfort. At moments of outrage at injustice, it gives hope. At moments of pain, it offers rest. But it also poses a challenge: in the light of the certain coming of Christ, how then should we live?

'Nice sermon, vicar!'

The start of today's reading introduces us to Amos – a farmer from the town of Tekoa, about 11 miles south of Jerusalem in the southern kingdom of Judah. He was not a professional priest, but someone who heard God's call to preach to the northern kingdom of Israel – not an easy task when people are likely to dismiss you as a foreigner who knows nothing. His ministry centred on Bethel, the place of worship where the movers and shakers of society met. He slots himself into the Bible time-line by telling us which kings were reigning north and south of the border – so we know his ministry took place midway through the eighth century before Jesus.

The book of Amos contains his sermon notes – and they tell us he was a passionate and fearless preacher. They are the notes of a man who studied his times, listened hard to God's voice and prepared well. And it is not a soft and gentle message that he brings (1:2); the Lord's voice, he says, is like that of a roaring lion. Amos grabs his audience's attention with a researched critique of the surrounding nations (1:3–2:3). Six of them are named and shamed for brutal acts of war, land-grabbing, the murder of innocents, treaty violations – even abusing the body of a dead king. His own homeland of Judah is not spared as their wilful rejection of God's law and embracing of false gods is brought under the spotlight (2:4–5).

You can imagine the congregation leaning forward with interest and revising their opinion of this southerner, warming to his message of judgment on these neighbours. But this was a sermon with a shock ending: Israel faced the righteous anger of God too (2:6–16). They had abused the poor, denied justice, allowed moral standards to slide and had sold out to materialism. They had forgotten the kindness of the Lord and had even sought to seduce and silence His messengers (2:10–12). They cannot escape the exile that awaits them, when all those things that gave them pleasure and pride and offered status and security would be stripped away.

You couldn't shake hands with Amos with a dismissive 'Nice sermon, vicar!'

Prepare to meet God

The verse which stands out for me from this reading reminds us that privilege carries responsibility (3:2). God had favoured Israel, yet Amos' indictment declares the people had slipped so far from His standards they could no longer tell right from wrong in everyday behaviour (3:10). Israel faced invasion by a foreign army and the exile of its people. This would happen within the lifetime of many of those who listened to Amos preach, and would be a wholesale defeat with only scraps remaining (3:12). The sanctuary at Bethel would be destroyed along with the holiday homes of the rich (3:14–15).

Amos pulls no punches as he likens the elegantly groomed wealthy women of high society to sleek cows. Their oppression of the poor and pursuit of self-centred pleasure will end with the humiliation of being dragged with ropes fastened to hooks inserted in their nose or lip (4:1–3) – the barbaric treatment handed out to prisoners of war. This preaching was very direct. Israel's religiosity had deafened its people to God's voice (4:4–5).

They had not given up on attending services or dropping their money in the plate – in fact they boasted about their generous giving. But they had failed to discern the Lord speaking through a series of what could be described as 'natural disasters'. Famine, drought, crop failure, locust plague, disease, military defeats and political problems had all been ignored (4:6–11). Yet these were an emergency call from God to the Israelites to get their lives straight. God will meet them – but not in the way they expect (4:12–13). Amos has the uncomfortable task of saying 'Time's up!'

Sometimes I make the foolish mistake of remarking, 'I wonder what the Lord is saying', as if He has a speech impediment of some kind. He has no communication problems, but I have reception difficulties. The Lord had spoken words of warning to Israel but the people had not tuned in to His voice.

Today's reading makes me think carefully about two issues fundamental to spiritual growth. First, that privilege carries responsibility, and second, that tuning in to the voice of the Lord is vital.

Stop the racket!

If you have shared a house with a child learning to play the violin you will know that not all music is relaxing! Sometimes it is more of a din than a concerto. This is how the Lord felt about the noisy worship songs at Israel's festivals (5:21–23), not because the people lacked musical talent but because they carried no credibility. Amos' message was clear: let justice and righteousness flow in daily life so worship songs are backed by actions (5:24).

Amos lamented as one would for a dead person (5:1) because he saw Israel heading for exile – broken, abandoned and unfulfilled (5:27). This was not the action of a vindictive God but the remedial discipline of a loving Father who still invites them to seek the Lord and live (5:4), and to change their ways by hating evil and loving good (5:14–15). The nation, however, had fallen a long way: the people despised truth and ignored those who challenged their behaviour (5:10); they trampled on the poor through exploitation (5:11); justice could be bought for those with cash, while those at the bottom of the ladder had no voice (5:12). It was no use speaking up or speaking out; if you were sensible you kept your mouth shut (5:12–13).

Two aspects of this spiritual slide are exposed. The first is complacency (6:1–7). A spiritual laziness had crept in, with leaders (who should have known better) indulging themselves with gourmet food and vintage wines while lounging in luxury. Yet they could not see how far from God the nation had drifted. The second trait was pride (6:8), which was rooted in the sense of being the chosen ones of Abraham's family, and manifested by resting secure in their military strength. Amos, with his prophetic eye, looks forward to a time not many years away when people will be reluctant to even mention the name of Yahweh because of the sense of fear it would evoke (6:9–10).

Complacency and pride are two themes that crop up in the Bible. They are obstacles to growth for a follower of Christ, so in your prayers today ask the Lord to search your heart and carry out any corrective surgery required (see Psa. 139:23–24).

Talking pictures

Some people are more visual than others – they see things in pictures rather than through words on a page. Amos was like that, and as he prepared to preach, God shaped his message by a series of visions – or talking pictures. These occurred during prayer times, and Amos lets us in on the dialogue between himself and the Lord.

First was a vision of a locust plague (7:1–3), then a fierce bush fire (7:4–6) – both potential acts of judgment the Lord declines to use. Then there came the builder's plumb-line (7:7–9), used to test that a wall is straight and true. Sadly, Israel failed the test. The last vision was that of a basket of ripe fruit. And the Lord showed Amos the nation was ripe for judgment – the time had come (8:1–2). Amos and his forthright preaching caused a stir, and Amaziah, a leading priest, accused him of plotting against the king and ordered him out of the country in derogatory terms (7:10–13).

Amos' reply is telling; his credentials are simply that God called him from farming and burned a message deep in his heart. He was not a paid professional but simply a man called by God to deliver a message (7:14–16). And part of that message was directed at Amaziah, outlining what would happen to his family (7:17).

We may find ourselves reacting against an apparently harsh message, but look at how far the people of Israel had fallen from the standards they had signed up to as Yahweh's covenant people. The poor were trampled on (8:4), merchants rushed through holy days to get back to making money (8:5), trading standards were ignored in the rush to make a quick buck (8:5), and people were bought and sold like cattle. God's judgment was righteous for these rebellious people who violated the covenant by their blatant materialism and exploitation of the poor. These were the very things the Lord had warned them against (see Deut. 15:1–11).

Judgment is inevitable, and Amos has another vision of a day fast approaching when there will be a famine, not of food, but of the Word of the Lord (8:11–12). People in exile desperate to hear some word of hope from God will hear only the sound of silence.

God is not **hungry**

IN ADDRESSING our underestimation of Him, God pinpoints two mistakes we make about Him.

Firstly, God summons His people to evaluate their worship, and, in particular, the value of the sacrifices that they make to Him.

It is unlikely that the psalmist is here repudiating all earlier biblical laws requiring ritual offerings. After all, God ordained them (v.8).

The point is: *He doesn't need them* (v.9).

'He owns "the cattle on a thousand hills" ' (v.10), words which I sang as a small child in Sunday school too long ago for polite memory to mention.

Everything belongs to God in the first place (vv.8–12). The promised land was always '*His* Land' of whom Israel was a tenant. The earth is the Lord's and we are all only undermanagers of *His* estate. What He desires from His worshippers is wise stewardship of the dominion He has delegated to us over His wonderful world.

The picture offered to us next is the comic image of a hungry God (v.12)! Even if He were to get hungry He wouldn't tell us because He can whistle up roast beef any time He chooses!

What He really hungers for are worshippers who give Him thanks, and pay their vows. Nothing pleases Him more than being called upon to live up to His name as Saviour of His people (vv.14–15).

Worshipping Him is not the sacrifice we make but the sacrifice we trust.

In short, God is never in our debt (cf. Isa. 40:13; Rom. 11:35).

The more we thank, the more we prepare the way for Him to show us more grace. The more we pay our vows the more indebted to grace we become (v.14).

We often hear it said: 'God has done so much for you: what will you do for Him?' Unfortunately, what this 'debtors' ethic' often means in practice, warns John Piper, is that 'good deeds and religious acts are the installment payments we make on the unending debt we owe God'.

As Piper memorably says, '*God will not surrender the glory of being the Giver.*'

No hiding place

Amos brought an uncompromising message, and predicted Israel would fall and its people be taken captive to a foreign land. History records this occurred in the year 722 BC when the Assyrian army invaded. The capital city of Samaria was destroyed, the whole country ravaged, and its people deported as slaves.

Significantly, it is the Lord Himself who stands by the altar in Amos' vision of the sanctuary at Bethel being brought crashing down (v.1). Yahweh chose to use the Assyrians as His tool (see Isa. 10:5); the calamity is of God's making.

There is no hiding place as God moves against His chosen people in judgment (vv.2–6). And in case we feel God is concerned only with Israel's behaviour, remember Amos' opening sermon (1:3–2:3); the whole world stands accountable before God (see Rom. 3:19). We do well to bear this in mind as we look at the news today and go about our tasks. The Lord is God of the whole earth. But notice how Amos' message concludes on a note of hope (vv.11–15). God's discipline is reme-dial, designed to bring change and growth. For the exiled people of Israel there was the promise that ruined cities would be rebuilt, crops harvested and the land restored (vv.14–15). But more than that, there is the promise of abundance. So great will be the fruitfulness of the soil that the reaper will be overtaken by the ploughman, anxious to sow the next crop (v.13).

It is difficult to read the words in verse 11 about David's tent being restored (his dwelling being rebuilt) without thinking of King David's greater son – the Lord Jesus Christ. Some rabbis believed this verse pointed towards the Messiah – the One who would be of David's family line and would sit on his throne. For Israel there was the promise of a new beginning; for all people there is the promise of a restored relationship with God through Christ.

As we conclude our studies in Amos I have been thinking about the man behind the message. Courage, obedience, a willingness to stand up and be counted, and going wherever the Lord sends are hallmarks of this man's devotion to his God. What an example!

The God who sees

The name Obadiah means 'servant, or worshipper, of the Lord', and that is all we know about the author of the shortest book in the Old Testament. We can't be completely certain when he lived, but if you consult a good Bible commentary you will discover the two main theories about the background to the book. However, this lack of definite information doesn't take away from Obadiah's powerful message.

The sermon is addressed to the people of Edom – one of Israel's nearest neighbours and, arguably, most bitter opponents. Despite strong family ties (the Edomites were descendants of Esau, the brother of Jacob; see Gen. 36:1), there had been centuries of bad blood between the two nations, much of which stemmed from the refusal of Edom to give the Israelites rights of passage when they left Egypt (see Num. 20:14–21).

Obadiah's message exposed the violence the Edomites showed towards the Israelites (v.10), including the slaughter of people seeking refuge (v.14). Obadiah refers to a specific incident when a marauding army attacked the Lord's people and the Edomites rejoiced (v.12). This callousness sprang from arrogance concerning their own power (v.3). Edom's capital, Sela, stood on a high rock, making it easy to defend. This gave the Edomites a false sense of security that the Lord was about to strip away (vv.4–9). The day of the Lord will be a day of reckoning for all nations (vv.15–21).

I am challenged by two thoughts. First, that the Lord is the all-seeing God (see Gen. 16:13), and no nation or individual in the long run will get away with anything (v.15). Second, I am struck by the truth that I am my brother's keeper – even when I don't like my brother very much! Edom rejoiced in Israel's misfortune, refused to help, joined in the slaughter, and profited into the bargain. Racial hatred and ethnic cleansing, tragically, have been around for centuries. The soil in which this kind of poisonous plant flourishes is a heart that is callous. Prejudice, unkind thoughts and a refusal to offer help are possibilities we face each day.

Lord, help me keep my heart clean.

Runaway

A reference to Jonah in an Old Testament history book sheds light on our reading (2 Kings 14:23–25). We discover Jonah prophesied during the reign of King Jereboam II of Israel (793–753 BC), lived just three miles from Nazareth, where Jesus would later grow up, and was a man with a good track record for fulfilled prophecies. So it is surprising that he deliberately disobeyed the Lord (v.3). Instead of going east to Nineveh, he headed west, 2,500 miles in the wrong direction.

Some have puzzled over why a prophet would say 'No' to the Lord he served well. A number suggest fear was the reason. Nineveh, the capital of Assyria, was an intimidating place. One Jewish writer described it as 'a symbol of evil incarnate'. Others put it down to Jonah's self-righteous attitude – he may have thought Nineveh deserved God's punishment. Then there is racism – perhaps Jonah just hated the Assyrians and wanted them to suffer. But notice that twice in one verse we are told Jonah was running away from God (v.3).

Abraham Maslow, the distinguished psychologist, coined the term the 'Jonah syndrome', and used it in connection with those who ran away from their responsibilities. Jonah's disobedience had implications that went beyond his private world (vv.4–6). In fear for their lives, his fellow travellers cast lots and discover Jonah is to blame for their calamity (v.7). He is honest enough to come clean and admit his failure (v.10), and even says that throwing him overboard is the best solution (v.12).

We are left with the challenging question: do I show symptoms of the 'Jonah syndrome'? Am I doing God's will, and doing it willingly? We may not jump on a boat, but there are other subtle ways to avoid responsibility. The fact is that others are affected by our actions. Even mature prophets face obedience issues, and I wonder if today we need to be reminded of the powerful message contained in Psalm 139.

We can run, but we can't hide. And, as Jonah discovered, God doesn't give up that easily. Obedience is always the best response to the call of the Lord.

Honest to God

Adversity often brings out the best. Jonah's uncomfortable stay in the belly of a great fish prompted the most honest prayer of his life. It was a prayer born out of desperation (2:1), totally honest in its admission of failure (2:2–6), and embraced decisiveness (2:7–9), signalling a new era in Jonah's walk of faith. In one of the most honest admissions in the Bible, Jonah admits you can't swim in the ocean of grace if you choose to paddle in the puddles of sin (2:8). And, from this honest-to-God conversation comes the commitment to do what God wants him to do (v.9). Jonah says 'Yes'.

Jonah is vomited into his ministry in what must be the most undignified entrance of any servant of the Lord (2:10). Notice 'The word of the LORD came to Jonah a second time' (3:1), reminding us that God is much more gracious than we are. Jonah was given an opportunity to put things right, which involved a gruelling 900-mile walk across desert roads in blazing sun. It would take a fit man six to seven weeks to complete the journey, so Jonah had a lot of time to think and pray.

Scholars have puzzled over the reference to a visit to Nineveh taking three days (3:3) since, although Nineveh was an important city, it was not that big. Some suggest the reference is to diplomatic protocol, when it would take an ambassador three days to complete the accepted civilities of presenting his credentials.

Jonah appeared in Nineveh as an emissary of the Lord of heaven and earth, and his message is condensed to a sound bite for the purposes of the book (3:4). Within six weeks, powerful, impregnable Nineveh would be overturned.

Jonah's assignment can be summarised in a word – tough. This may give a clue to his original reluctance. It was no easy thing to make an arduous journey and deliver an uncomfortable message to the most powerful city on earth. Foreigners are often regarded with suspicion, and criticising one's hosts is never a wise move. But God found in Jonah a willing heart – even if he took some time to get there.

Honest prayers and rugged obedience make strong men and women of faith.

The great God

G Campbell Morgan, a famous preacher, wrote, 'Men have looked so hard at the great fish they have failed to see the great God.' When we consider that the whole book of Jonah consists of just 48 verses, and God is mentioned in 39 of them, we can see his point.

The stunning response of the people of Nineveh (3:5–8) is not as far from our experience as we may think. Recall the aftermath of the death of the Princess of Wales and remember the national mood of grief and confusion. History records that around the time of Jonah's visit three events occurred in Nineveh in a six-year time frame. A major plague was followed by a solar eclipse (seen as a sign of the gods' displeasure), then a second plague rocked the city. Jonah's message fell like a seed on ploughed soil.

But more astonishing than the repentance of the Ninevites is the spiritual sulk that swamped Jonah (4:1–3). God's mercy towards the city had not gone down well with His servant. And this remarkable little book concludes with a living parable about a vine,

a worm and a grumpy prophet with sunstroke (4:4–11).

Here is the heart of the book: God is a missionary who cares desperately about people of *all* nationalities, and their welfare matters to Him (v.11). This was shocking stuff to those Jews who rested on their laurels of election and showed disdain for the surrounding nations. Jonah is a mirror image of that kind of 'couldn't-care-less' attitude that exists in far too many churches. We would do well to reflect deeply about what this book reveals to us of our great God.

Thomas Carlisle sums up the challenging implications of the message of Jonah.

And Jonah stalked
To his shaded seat
And waited for God
To come round to his way of thinking
And God is still waiting for a host of
  Jonahs
In their comfortable houses
To come around
To his way of loving.

Quoted by Donald E. Messer,
A Conspiracy of Goodness
(Nashville: Abingdon, 1992) p.75.

The Godness of **God**

THIS PSALM rebuts the notion that our religious activity plugs some gap in God's resources (v.9). As has been well said: 'Even if all the prodigal sons came home on the same day that would not put the Father in an embarrassing position.'

Furthermore, we mistakenly assume that if only we prayed or fasted more, then God would be obliged to bless us! But God is under obligation to no one but Himself.

In any case, our God is *far less religious than we are.*

He exposes – as His prophets typically do – His people's hypocritical separation of worship and work.

The people condemned here are those who recite the Ten Commandments in worship and break them in the workplace and the bedroom (vv.18–20).

Again the failure is to *underestimate* God.

We misread His patience with us as His conniving at our insincerity; His silence as acquiescence in our double-lives (v.21). But God is not the unseen guest at every transaction who for all practical purposes we can ignore. Suddenly He shows up!

We think He is a silent spectator of all our double-dealing. Now He speaks!

The fact that God does graciously condescend to represent Himself to us with human characteristics and feelings must not lead us to devalue His deity.

It is just here that He re-asserts His '*God*ness' (cf. Hos. 11:9). In holiness, in faithfulness, He is most decidedly *not like us* (v.21). God refuses to be remade in our image, or presumed upon to 'nod and wink' at our blatant insincerity.

When the real God re-appears it's more a slap in the face than a pat on the back (v.21b). God is no church-mouse but the lion that roars and tears (v.22). Covenant-breakers beware.

And yet, the God who comes in such splendour and with such penetrating analysis, comes, not to abolish our worship, but to cleanse and renew it. A new way of worship is offered to us in which to honour Him rightly opens the way for further displays of His amazing grace. Who would want to underestimate Him whose final word is 'salvation' (v.23)?

The only Time Lord

Jonah and Nahum shared the same job – but 150 years apart. Nahum (the name means 'comfort') was called to preach about the impending downfall of Nineveh and the Assyrian empire. This was the dominant world superpower, infamous for its cruelty, and the window of mercy opened in Jonah's time was now shut.

Nahum's message begins with a stunning description of God's character (1:2–7). We may struggle with words such as 'jealous and avenging' (1:2) because we view them from our own fallen standpoint. There is a good side to jealousy. This is God's world and He has every right to call the shots and make the rules. He is good and a refuge for those who seek Him (v.7), but an opponent to all who would proudly defy His rule.

The strong, all-conquering Assyrian armies were based in Nineveh. Yet they would be destroyed within a few years of Nahum's preaching (1:9–15). Though the northern kingdom of Israel had fallen to these armies in 722 BC, Nahum prophesied that the conqueror would be conquered. There can be no more chilling message to hear than that the Lord stands against you (2:13).

The week I am writing this the United Nations General Assembly has been meeting in New York. Political analysts have been debating the balance of global power and assessing where the world is heading. It is interesting to read Nahum's prophecy with current affairs at the forefront of my mind. Paul preached to the intellectuals at Athens concerning the one and only Time Lord who governs the history of all peoples (Acts 17:26). It is good to be reminded where the real power lies. It is not in Washington, Beijing, Moscow or London, but in the courts of heaven.

Many use the words of the Lord's prayer every day. Today's reading helps us pray with greater understanding, 'Your kingdom come, your will be done on earth as it is in heaven' (Matt. 6:10).

Let this truth invade your prayers today as you commit the world and your small part in it to the Lord. To many of Nahum's listeners the thought of Assyria stripped of power seemed impossible. But they hadn't reckoned on the Lord of History.

Inhumanity to man

There are countless incidents in history of what we describe as 'man's inhumanity to man'. Every generation produces examples of human depravity at its worst. The Assyrians were one such example, and they inflicted gruesome punishments on the peoples they conquered. Nahum's final words sum it up: few had escaped their endless cruelty (v.19). His book is elegantly written and full of vivid imagery. The first chapter is an acrostic poem, and each verse begins with the next letter of the Hebrew alphabet. This made Nahum's message easy to memorise and recall.

Reading today's passage is like watching a TV news report: soldiers, horses, plunder, prisoners and dead bodies whirl around in Nahum's wordscape (vv.1-4). Then there is the image of proud Assyria pelted in the stocks like a common prostitute (vv.4-5).

Nahum knew history, and showed it by referring to a famous Assyrian victory over the Egyptian city of Thebes. The Assyrians had mercilessly destroyed the city and killed many of its inhabitants in 663 BC (vv.8-10).

For all its power, Thebes fell – and Nahum declares the same fate would befall Assyria and its proud capital of Nineveh.

Nahum adds that the injury to be inflicted by the hand of the Lord will be fatal (v.19). This prediction was fulfilled in 612 BC. Nineveh was totally destroyed and never rebuilt. Within a few centuries the ruins were covered by sand blown from the desert. The site was discovered by an English archaeologist in the 1820s on the banks of the Tigris river, some 250 miles north of Baghdad in Iraq. The Bible declares, 'It is a dreadful thing to fall into the hands of the living God' (Heb. 10:31), and Nahum's stark message reveals the truth of this solemn statement.

I am left with two striking thoughts. First, Nahum assures me that God does put wrongs right. Second, he challenges me to ensure my beliefs and behaviour match. It is no use being intensely spiritual and holy minded if kindness, courtesy, forgiveness, mercy and practical care are absent from my life. There is no excuse for man's inhumanity to man.

The **Big Picture**

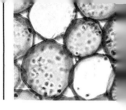

Philip Greenslade gives us a glimpse of how the Minor Prophets and Ephesians fit together in God's story.

Separated as they are by some 800 years, the Minor Prophets and Ephesians are, nevertheless, part of the same spectrum of faith and revelation. Separated even more crucially by the climactic event of Jesus Christ, they are, nonetheless, on the same timeline of grace.

The Old Testament prophets vigorously contribute to God's earlier phase of revelation which steers history forward to the gift of Jesus. The apostolic letters offer their distinctive and authoritative witness, reflecting on the impact and significance of Christ not just for themselves, but for that earlier phase of God's dealings with the world through His people Israel. Inspired foresight is matched by inspired hindsight, and each helps to interpret the other.

Hosea, for example, comes closer than any other Old Testament prophet – Jeremiah apart – to personally anticipating the incarnation and sufferings of Jesus. Hosea embodied this message, his own tragic love life becoming a painful parable of God's broken heart over His 'bride', Israel.

As H.H. Rowley said of Hosea, 'Not by the things that he saw, but by the things that he suffered, he was lifted into the heart of God'. And all this was in prophetic service to the emotional commitment of God (Hos. 11) to His redeemed people and to His larger redemptive plan.

**THE LINKING OF ...
PROPHETS AND ...
APOSTLES ACROSS
EIGHT CENTURIES ONLY
SERVES TO SHOW HOW
BREATHTAKING IS THE
SCOPE OF GOD'S STRATEGY**

The linking of Old Testament prophets and New Testament apostles across eight centuries only serves to show how breathtaking is the scope of God's strategy. In Eugene Peterson's stirring paraphrase, God 'set it all out before us in Christ, a *long-range plan* in which everything would be brought together and summed up in him, everything in

Dear friend,

I wanted to share with you a recent development for CWR which is both exciting and significant, and comes during **2012, the 25th anniversary of the opening of Waverley Abbey House**. It is here that marriages have been mended, burnt-out leaders restored, people healed and envisioned, professionals and counsellors trained, and thousands brought to a fresh understanding and enthusiasm for God's Word. Many have established ministries of their own both in the UK and overseas: the ripple effect is awesome!

One thing that drew me to CWR and its founders, Selwyn Hughes and Trevor Partridge, was their reputation for **combining biblical insight with practical application**. They were energised by a vision of equipping men and women of conviction and character to help change the face of contemporary society – and the **establishing of a Christian university**.

Our BA in Christian Counselling has now received full university validation. The positive uptake of the course and high student numbers has heightened the need for increased space. **Waverley Abbey House will be full to capacity by the end of 2012.**

We need your help ...

... and the need is urgent

Additional space is needed in order to accommodate our increasing numbers of students, build on our existing programmes and develop a place of learning and education for key influencers in society: lawyers, politicians, educators, health professionals, those working in the media and captains of industry – equipping them to be a godly influence in their everyday workplaces.

An unexpected opportunity

An unexpected door opened in 2011 when an existing Christian conference centre, **Pilgrim Hall** (in East Sussex) became available, offering 12 acres of land, 110 beds, a lift enabling access to all floors and adaptable conferencing and teaching facilities.

I ask you to invest with us so that Pilgrim Hall's **rich Christian heritage will not be lost** to the Christian community and we will be enabled to develop new university-accredited programmes such as teacher education and other vocational qualifications. These would be offered with **strong biblical foundations** within an environment of **spiritual growth and discipleship**, where individuals studying their chosen vocations and professions are fully integrated with biblical ethics, values and understanding.

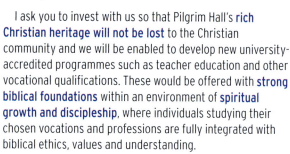

Help us establish a Christian College of Education leading to a Christian university

The total cost of Pilgrim Hall, including refurbishing, refitting, financing tutorial staff and sustaining the project **is £3 million – substantially less than developing comparable facilities at Waverley Abbey House**.

With a combination of donations and loans from CWR Partners and supporters we have raised £1.5 million. A further £1.5 million is needed, **with our next deadline due in September this year.**

I have calculated that if each of us were able to **invest just £50** or 5,000 invested £100, 2,500 invested £200 or 1,000 invested £500, we could reach our urgent target.

I ask that you prayerfully consider joining with us so that, God willing, with your help, **Waverley will become the pivotal hub** from which Christian campuses can be established in this country and beyond - training, supporting and educating a generation of nation changers, **a place of revival and refreshing from which God's living water can flow out to a dry and thirsty world**.

May I thank you on behalf of the board and all the staff for your generosity; together we will be part of something 'more than we can possibly imagine ...'

Sincerely yours in His name

Mick Brooks

Yes, I want to invest with others, so that together we will be part of something more than we can possibly imagine ...

Gift amount:

☐ **£50**

☐ **£100** I want to be 1 in 5,000

☐ **£200** I want to be 1 in 2,500

☐ **£500** I want to be 1 in 1,000

£_____ Preferred amount

For more information or to donate online go to www.cwr.org.uk/ph

☐ Please send me an acknowledgement of my gift.

Once funds have been raised to meet the immediate needs of this appeal, CWR reserves the right to use any monies received to fund other Bible-based ministry around the world.

YOUR DETAILS (REQUIRED FOR ORDERS AND DONATIONS)

Name:	**CWR ID No.** (if known):
Home Address:	
	Postcode:
Telephone No. (for queries):	**Email:**

GIFT AID (YOUR HOME ADDRESS REQUIRED, SEE ABOVE)

giftaid it

I am a UK taxpayer and want CWR to reclaim the tax on all my donations for the four years prior to this year **and on** all donations I make from the date of this Gift Aid declaration until further notice.*

Taxpayer's Full Name (IN BLOCK CAPITALS) _____

Signature _____ **Date** _____

*I understand I must pay an amount of Income/Capital Gains Tax at least equal to the tax the charity reclaims in the tax year.

PAYMENT DETAILS

☐ I enclose a cheque/PO made payable to CWR for the amount of: **£** _____

☐ Please charge my credit/debit card.

Cardholder's name (in BLOCK CAPITALS) _____

Card No. | ☐☐☐☐ | ☐☐☐☐ | ☐☐☐☐ | ☐☐☐☐ | ☐☐☐

Expires end ☐☐ ☐☐

Security Code ☐☐☐

CWR Applying God's Word *to everyday life and relationships*

CWR, Waverley Abbey House, Waverley Lane, Farnham, Surrey GU9 8EP

CWR is a registered charity No. 294387 and a limited company registered in England No. 1990308

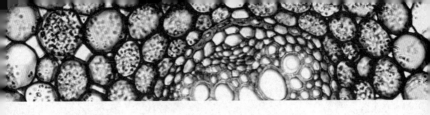

deepest heaven, everything on planet earth' (Eph. 1:9–10, *The Message*).

In writing the letter to the Ephesians, Paul presents a brilliant summary of his conviction that 'in Christ' *the mystery of God's will for the world* is, in fact, no longer a mystery at all but is now an open secret – the shared secret of God's plan of salvation. Everything in God's saving plan finally centres on Jesus (Eph. 3:4), whose mystery is made know in the gospel. And for Paul the gospel is an '*idea whose time has come*'.

EVERYTHING IN GOD'S SAVING PLAN FINALLY CENTRES ON JESUS

Paul makes clear that this was *not* revealed to previous generations as 'it has now been revealed by the Spirit to God's holy apostles and prophets' (Eph. 3:5).

Just as God's 'secret', disclosed only through His prophets (Amos 3:7), became foundational Scripture so, by analogy, and also by the Holy Spirit, those who receive and transmit the 'mystery' of God – namely the New Testament apostles and the prophetic figures associated with them – lay the foundation for the New Testament as authoritative Scripture (Eph. 2:20).

Furthermore, both Old Testament prophets and New Testament apostles are partners in God's intention to call out a people worthy of His name, Gentiles included (cf. Amos 9:11–15; Hos. 2:23).

Just as the prophets strove to recall the people of Israel to their true covenant identity and vocation, so Paul works tirelessly to conform the Church to the shape of Christ. Such an 'ekklesia' will be a home for both Jew and Gentile (Eph. 3:3–6) and an advance sample of what a new human race will look like (Eph. 2:13–19).

Judged by the stature of God's full and final Apostle and Prophet, Jesus Christ (Eph. 4:7ff), we may well feel ourselves to be very '*minor*' prophets. But, far from diminishing us, this realisation in fact ennobles us since we are all destined, in God's long-range plan, to grow up to the measure of His maturity.

Ephesians
Peter Hicks

LIKE MOST of Paul's letters, Ephesians touches on dozens of great themes, any one of which would repay a month's study. But as we read through this letter this month we're going to let its greatest theme tie all our study together. That theme can be summed up in one word that Paul uses in chapter 1 verse 10, translated in the NIV as 'together under one head'.

Division, rejection, fragmentation, hostility, separation, loneliness, alienation – these are key features of our world. In response to each of them God speaks the word 'together'. Reconciliation, love, unity, acceptance, peace – these are His vision and His gift, and they're the theme of this great letter.

Rebellion, rejection of God as God, the insistence that we run our lives and our planet our own way – that's the source of all that is evil in the world today. To that, God has the answer: to bring all things together 'under one head'. And that one head is the Lord Jesus Christ.

Everything 'together under one head' is God's vision and purpose for planet Earth. As we work through this letter He's going to be calling us again to make sure that it's a reality in our own lives, and challenging us to be the people through whom it becomes a reality in the world around us. Be ready to hear His voice; be open to be challenged and changed by the riches of this section of His Word.

Peter Hicks

What God has done

Are you a marveller? Again and again in his letters Paul marvels at what God has done. Excitement, joy and praise well up in him and burst out into his writing (v.3).

If you're like me, you may feel you've lost much of the art of marvelling. Perhaps we've become so familiar with the truths of what God has done that they no longer make our hearts beat faster and praise burst from our lips. If so, today's an opportunity to put that right. How about making time to work through these seven steps?

1. Pray that 'the eyes of your heart may be enlightened' by 'the Spirit of wisdom and revelation' (vv.17–18).

2. Select just one great thing God has done for you. It could be one of the things Paul lists in verses 4–8, or something else special for you.

3. Spend a few minutes reflecting where you'd be today if God hadn't done this thing for you. (See how Paul does this in chapter 2 verses 1–3

and 11–12.) Write down a summary of your reflections.

4. Next, write a short sentence starting 'But God …'

5. In contrast to step 3, write down the difference 'But God …' has made.

6. Spend time rejoicing. You could use a psalm like Psalm 30 or 34, or a hymn or song of thanksgiving and praise.

7. All day keep going back to your 'But God …' Write it on the back of your hand or on a card to remind you, and each time let it lift your heart in praise.

Praise, my soul, the King of heaven,
To His feet thy tribute bring.
Ransomed, healed, restored, forgiven,
Who like thee His praise should sing?
Praise Him! Praise Him!
Praise Him! Praise Him!
Praise the everlasting King!
Henry Francis Lyte

What God is going to do

Think of anything – today's news, your circumstances, the devil, your experiences, Islam, suffering, politics, art, history, protons, galaxies – good, bad, big, small, past, future. God has a plan, an amazing God-sized plan for everything. Because it's God-sized it's bound to be a 'mystery' to us (v.9). But, marvels Paul, it's been the 'good pleasure' of our God to make known this plan, not telling us all the details, for that would be far too complex to grasp, but revealing to us His great overarching purpose and goal.

That goal hasn't yet been achieved. But He's working everything towards it. One day, 'when the times will have reached their fulfilment' (v.10), the last pieces of the jigsaw will be put in place and the final picture will be complete.

The key to that plan, as the key to the blessings listed in verses 3–8, is Christ (v.9). And the plan itself is nothing less than 'to bring all things in heaven and on earth together under one head, even Christ' (v.10).

When Paul says 'all things' he means 'all things'. Whatever happens, whatever you can think of, it's God's purpose to bring it under the headship or lordship of Christ. How He'll do it may still be a mystery, but *that* He'll do it is an absolute certainty. In a sense He's already done it (v.22), since Christ's total lordship has already been demonstrated by His resurrection and ascension (vv.20–21). Though still to us much in the world seems meaningless and chaotic and hopeless, it's not that way for God, and one day we, and all creation, will marvel at the glory and wisdom of how He's fitted it into His plan (Rev. 15:3; Phil. 2:10–11).

'All things' includes me and you (vv.11–14). So everything that happens to us is ultimately under the headship of Christ; however hard it is for us to see it now, in the fullness of God's plan, over everything Jesus is Lord. What's more, already today He calls us to share in His plan by consciously putting everything – thoughts, actions, attitudes, ambitions, worries, feelings, everything we are or do – under His headship.

What God wants to do now

God's amazing plan is to bring everything in the universe together under the headship of Christ. We're part of that plan; our lives are part of its fulfilment.

In this prayer Paul asks for three things he knew God wants to do in His people: Try selecting just one of these today; think about its implications; set your heart on it; remove any barriers in its way; cry to God with all your being, 'Lord, through "the Spirit of wisdom and revelation" (v.17) do this in me today.'

1. A deepening relationship with our 'glorious Father' (v.17). Separation, alienation, division and the like are rife in our broken world, but reconciliation, restoration and a deep relationship of oneness and love are what God has made possible for His people through Christ. For us the greatest part of His awesome purpose to bring all things together is the bringing of rebellious sinners like us into a relationship of love and oneness with a holy God.

2. A richer awareness, in theory and in practice, of what it means to be a Christian (v.18). Too often we settle for a pale reflection of the real thing: we see being a Christian as accepting a set of beliefs or following a certain lifestyle, while in fact it is being blessed 'with every spiritual blessing in Christ' (v.3), living as sons and daughters of God Himself (v.5), and experiencing all the riches that this entails, both now and in the future (v.18).

3. Power for God's people. There are many forms of power that we as God's people must turn away from, such as power that exalts us or demeans others. But there's one power, perhaps only one, that we're called to hunger after: the power of God at work in and through us (v.19). This is the amazing power that raised Jesus from the dead and will, in God's time, bring all things under Christ as head.

To cry out for this power is to cry 'Your kingdom come'; it is a longing that God will work in power in and through us to demonstrate for all to see that Jesus is Lord.

'All **blessing** and **all-blest**'

HOW REMARKABLE that we can bless God! This classic Jewish tradition of prayers that begin with '*berakah*' or 'blessed be' shows up at the end of each of the five books of psalms. Today's psalm probably originated in a liturgical setting.

It envisages a round-the-clock activity (v.1b) originally the privilege of the Levitical 'servants of the LORD', the priestly leaders of worship in Israel (cf. 1 Chron. 23:30).

Whoever offers 'blessing' to God gathers up into one the response of a grateful people and creation, and offers it back 'with interest' to the God who gives so lavishly.

Of course, in 'blessing' God we do not *add* anything to God's fullness and sufficiency. In Derek Kidner's words, 'The exchange is unequal; to bless God is to acknowledge gratefully what he is; but to bless man, God must make him what he is not, and give him what he has not.'

So the psalm which opens with 'blessing' directed to God (vv.1–2) ends with the blessing returning from God to us in a classic 'benediction' (v.3).

In this classic biblical rhythm of grace, God is to be 'blessed ... because he has blessed us ...' (cf. Eph. 1:1–14, though the NIV unfortunately misses the connection by translating *eulogeo* which means 'to bless' by the more general term 'to praise'). But don't let's miss the vital connection being made by the psalmist (and Paul).

If our blessing God adds nothing to His glory it may nevertheless *complete* something important in His relationship to His creation.

In William Hendricksen's words, 'Gratitude is that which completes the circle whereby blessing returns to the Giver in the form of unending adoration.'

Here occurs what Daniel Hardy and David Ford call 'the ecology of blessing'. In this ecosystem of love, the love which flows out of God to us and back to Him again in praise and worship is the love that 'returns all reality to God, and so let's all be taken up into the spiral of mutual appreciation and delight which is the fulfilment of creation'.

'But God ...' (1)
From death to resurrection life

Last Wednesday we reflected on where we'd be if God hadn't worked in our lives, and how 'But God ...' has made all the difference. For the next three days we'll pick up the theme of 'But God ...' and unpack some of the radical changes that have come about as God has put His great plan into operation in our lives.

If Christ isn't our Head, something else must be. The New Testament describes this alternative power in various ways; verses 1 to 3 speak of 'transgressions and sins', 'this world', 'the ruler of the kingdom of the air', and 'the cravings of our sinful nature'. Perhaps it doesn't really matter what we call it; the horrific fact is, that, if we don't have God in Christ as Head and Lord in our lives, the power that will control us is the anti-God power of evil, the opposite of all that God is, the power that is under His righteous 'wrath' (v.3) and judgment, the power that holds us in death (vv.2,5).

'But ... God ... made us alive' (v.5). Into the corpses He breathed His life. The chains of death and hell and Satan and sin were broken by the power of Christ's resurrection (1:20–21). As Christ was raised and exalted to the position of headship in the universe, so God 'raised us up with Christ and seated us with him in the heavenly realms in Christ Jesus' (v.6).

Why? For many reasons. Because He loved us and because He's rich in mercy, for a start (v.4). Then, on a more practical note, to demonstrate to everyone the astounding riches of His grace (v.7), and to transform us from sinners to those whose lives radiate His goodness (v.10).

How are you doing on those last two? Do the people who know you, not to mention the hosts of angels who are watching you, see how you live and burst out with 'praise of his glorious grace' (1:6)? And how are you getting on with those 'good works' (v.10) that God has called you to, not to earn salvation (vv.8–9), but to demonstrate the reality of the One who is now Head and Lord in your life?

'But God ...' (2)
From 'far' to 'near'

As a well-taught Jew, Paul had been convinced that non-Jews didn't stand a chance when it came to having a relationship with God. His catalogue of words and images to describe their condition is horrific: 'separate', 'excluded', 'foreigners', 'without hope', 'without God', 'barrier', 'dividing wall of hostility', 'aliens' (vv.12,14,19). They are all summed up in those two words 'far away' (v.13).

But the opposite of 'far away' is very near. In His grace God has brought very near to Himself both Jews, who thought they were near already but still needed the gospel of peace (v.17), and non-Jews who, without the gospel, would have remained 'without hope and without God in the world' (v.12).

The implications of being 'near' to God are many; Paul lists some in verses 19–22. Here's a checklist taken from John's Gospel of some of the ways we can assess how near our lives *really* are to our Saviour and God.

• Do I stick with Him when the going gets tough? (John 6:66–69)

• Do the rivers of the Spirit flow from within me? (John 7:37–39)

• Do I walk in the light? (John 8:12; 3:21)

• Do I hear the voice of Jesus and follow Him? (John 10:27)

• Do I demonstrate love to other Christians as Jesus has demonstrated love to me? (John 13:34–35)

• Do I obey the commands of Jesus? (John 14:15)

• Is God at home in me? (John 14:23)

• Is my life marked by the peace and joy of Jesus? (John 14:27; 15:11)

• Do I bear much fruit? (John 15:4–5)

'But God ...' (3)
From division to unity

On Monday we saw how 'But God ...' revolutionised our personal condition. Yesterday 'But God ...' revolutionised our relationship with Him. Today's 'But God ...' brings about a revolution in a third area, that of our relationship with other Christians. God is working to fulfil His amazing plan of bringing all things together under one head, and one of the ways He's doing it is by calling a very mixed bag of people into a relationship with Himself and so with each other.

Three times in verse 6 Paul uses the word 'together' in describing the revolution in relationships between Jews and Gentiles brought about by accepting the gospel. It is God's purpose that Jews and Gentiles – two groups as polarised as any groups today – should be 'heirs together', 'members together of one body', and 'sharers together in the promise in Christ Jesus'.

Praise God for all the progress that has been made in bringing together all the disparate groups that God has chosen to make up His people. But still there's so much that must grieve His heart. He may not worry particularly about the structures that keep us apart (I have a suspicion that His interest in ecclesiastical structures is pretty minimal), but what hurts Him is our attitudes and our actions. When, instead of accepting one another and loving one another despite our differences, we criticise, reject and ignore each other, the Spirit who has made us one is grieved. When we are quicker to judge and condemn than to make allowances and show grace, God looks in vain for 'the likeness of his Son' (Rom. 8:29) in us.

'Together' is God's word. Even when we try to justify our apartness by theological arguments or our fear of compromising doctrinal purity or the concept that we can do better on our own than by working with others, God's word is still 'together'. When we're with Him in glory we'll be together with all His people, from all backgrounds, all brands of theology, all styles of church practice, all ways of doing things. His word for us today is 'together'. If we're one with Him now we must be one with each other.

One together (1)
Putting Satan's nose out of joint

Like all these early chapters of Ephesians this passage is packed with profound truths. We'll focus on just one of them, picking up again the theme of God's 'eternal purpose which he accomplished in Christ Jesus our Lord' (v.11) and our high calling to demonstrate and make it known.

Though it caused him suffering and cost him his freedom (v.1), Paul saw the calling to tell others about the purposes of God through the gospel as a gracious gift from God (vv.1,7,8). But he wasn't the only one to whom God has given this gift; the calling to express the good news of God's purposes is one shared by all 'the church' (v.10), that is, all the people of God.

God calls His people to demonstrate and declare His purposes to all; but verse 10 specifically mentions that we are to do it to 'the rulers and authorities in the heavenly realms'. These could well be great angelic beings, such as are referred to in 1 Peter 1:12, but it also seems likely to include 'the spiritual forces of evil in the heavenly realms' that Paul writes about in Ephesians 6:12.

Here is a staggering truth. It is through us and what we are that the powers of evil come to see 'the manifold wisdom of God' (v.10). Perhaps their intelligence is insufficient to cope with the profound complexity of the purposes of God; perhaps they have refused to accept them, choosing to kid themselves that God's love and power aren't big enough to break the hold of sin and evil and division on human lives. Either way, they can't grasp the reality of what God has done in bringing all things together in Christ – until they see it in us. But when they do see it, it's the stroke of doom for them, the evidence that God's power and love have triumphed over evil.

Five times in this letter Paul states that as children of God our lives have an impact in the heavenly realms. No longer is it 'you in your small corner and I in mine'. 'Through the working of his power' (v.7) every day together we are part of our God's cosmic victory.

One together (2)
Filled with the love of God

God, in His 'manifold wisdom', is already using His people to demonstrate to 'the rulers and authorities in the heavenly realms' (v.10) His great plan to bring all things together under one head, the Lord Jesus Christ. But such a demonstration will carry little weight if in reality God's people are all at sixes and sevens, lacking that very oneness that is God's goal. Because of this Paul includes a second prayer in this letter, a prayer that has love at its heart. Later in the letter he's going to call his readers to 'live a life of love' (5:2); here in this prayer he recognises that we can only live love if we first experience love, the love of God in Christ.

Do you find love a problem? Is there someone you find hard to love? Do you have difficulty receiving love from others? Or do you feel unloved, rejected, perhaps, by those you feel should love you, or even rejected by God? Today, God gives you this beautiful prayer, with the assurance that as you pray it His amazing power will work in you for His glory (vv.20–21).

Here are some truths to feed upon as you pray this prayer.

• God the Father is love (v.14; 1 John 4:7–8). Even the deepest bonds of love within a human family are no more than a pale reflection of the burning love of our heavenly Father.

• God the Spirit pours His love into our 'inner being' 'with power' (v.16; Rom. 5:5).

• God the Son is living in our hearts (v.17).

• Love is our foundation. The tense Paul uses for 'being rooted and established in love' (v.17) indicates that we already have our roots deep in the love of God; our lives are already firmly established on His love. This is His doing, and we can be sure of it.

• Because God is in us, God's love is in us, and it's vast, big enough for anything (vv.18–19).

• Amazingly, through the grace and power of God, we can 'know', not just intellectually but in experience, the vastness and fullness of this love, even though it 'surpasses knowledge' (v.19).

Praise has its **reasons**

PRAISE IS never meant to be a mindless activity. Whether exuberant or solemn, our songs should always reveal the real *reasons* for our praise.

This common feature of Israel's praise is neatly illustrated in this, the shortest psalm, which hinges on the small word 'for' (v.2). Praise and extol the Lord 'for' ... in this case 'for' His great love towards us. In true praise we are not looking *inward*, monitoring and mentioning our own fleeting feelings, but looking *upward*, mindful of, and grateful for, God's enduring faithfulness.

Our songs and prayers, our kneeling and dancing – all we do 'before the Lord' – needs always to be a reasonable and reasoned response to what God has done for us.

Worship, however lively, should never be merely a matter of 'having a good time'. Even less should it be the enduring of a boring ritual with our conscious thoughts absent and on something else.

No: for the psalmist, praising God was a heartfelt, active, expressive appreciation for what God had done for His people.

For Israel there was no celebration without victory. And if Israel's praise was inward grace turned upward in gratitude, then it was also turned *outward* in prophetic expression of a world-view (v.1). 'In the regular repeated action of praise,' says Walter Brueggemann, 'the community engages in an act of imagination that keeps the wondrous world of Yahweh's good governance available and credible.' This summary song, he adds, 'keeps alive a vision of all peoples gathered in one act of worship'.

All nations are invited to celebrate at the feast which the One Creator God in love and faithfulness has spread before His whole creation.

'With offerings of devotion
Ships from the isles shall meet,
To pour the wealth of oceans,
In tribute at his feet.'
James Montgomery

When, as Christians, we contemplate what God has done in Jesus Christ, for His whole world, we surely need no other reasons to persuade us to rejoice. Hallelujah.

One together (3)
Unity in practice

God has called us to declare and demonstrate His great plan to bring all things together under one head, the Lord Jesus Christ. So it is our task 'to live a life worthy of the calling' we've received (v.1).

Paul uses the word 'one' no fewer than seven times in these verses – eight times if you include his word 'one-ness' translated by the NIV as 'unity' in verse 3. Jesus used the same word five times in His great prayer for unity in John 17. Our relationship of unity, said Jesus, must be modelled on His relationship of oneness with His Father (John 17:21). Paul calls us to unity because oneness is the hallmark of just about everything there is in the Christian gospel (vv.4–6).

Some have interpreted this passage as applying exclusively to interdenominational unity but, although that's a valid and important application, the primary thrust of these verses is a call to oneness in the local church, to true love and unity with all our Christian neighbours. In verses 2 and 3 Paul suggests five practical steps we can take to fulfil that call.

1. Accept unity as a given. It's not something we have to create; there *is* 'one body and one Spirit' and so on (v.4). Despite our many differences we *are* one with each other. God has given us oneness in the Spirit; our task is to accept it and 'keep' it, to make sure we do nothing to destroy it (v.3).

2. Work hard at maintaining unity. 'Make every effort' (v.3). Go out of your way to heal breaches.

3. Be 'completely humble' (v.2). Be the first to apologise, to admit your faults, to give way.

4. Be 'gentle' (v.2). Never fall to the temptation to trample on someone else, to put them down, show how foolish or wrong they are, or to score points over them. Treat them as graciously as you know Jesus will treat you.

5. Be 'patient' or, more literally, long-suffering, 'bearing with one another in love' (v.2). Put up with anything; don't rise to the bait; show how much the love of God in you can take and forgive.

One together (4)
Unity in diversity

Here's some bad logic: 'In our church we've got the most explosive mix you could imagine: traditionalists and radicals, pentecostals and reformed, high-flying professionals and very ordinary non-professionals, young and old, and people from all sorts of ethnic and cultural backgrounds. The sparks are certainly going to fly.'

Here's some much better logic: 'We too have a very broad mix in our church. We see this as a sign of God's grace towards us in giving us an opportunity to grow together towards maturity. Great things are going to happen.'

Like Romans 12 and 1 Corinthians 12–14, this passage speaks of the variety of gifts God gives His people (v.11). At Corinth this variety was allowed to cause disunity, but here Paul emphasises that God's intention is the opposite; it should be used to build up God's people 'until we all reach unity in the faith and in the knowledge of the Son of God' (vv.12–13).

What these verses say about the variety of gifts, we can extend to the variety of backgrounds or cultures or ways of seeing things that we find in our churches. The Lord of the Church knows what He's doing when He puts such a varied group together; He's implementing His great plan to bring all things together under one head, even Christ, and He's giving us an opportunity to work with Him. That man who's so different from me and whom I struggle to cope with isn't a problem put into the church by the devil; he's a gift from God to enrich others, and me in particular, with his distinctive approach. That woman who seems to delight in being awkward is a gift from God to help us all grow in patience and understanding and grace and love.

'Impossible,' you say. 'Differences and difficult people are bound to lead to problems and upsets and division. It always happens that way.'

Perhaps so, if we leave God out of it. But most definitely not so, if we allow the One, who was able to bring together under one head Jew and Gentile, to be truly Lord of our church and our lives.

One together (5)
More unity in practice

On Monday we looked at five practical steps suggested by the opening verses of this chapter that we should be taking to ensure that nothing destroys God's great purpose of unity in His people. Today we can add five more.

6. Recognise that we're all different (v.7). God hasn't chosen to establish monochrome churches. He's a God of variety.

7. Our calling is to serve each other. Paul has already called himself a 'servant' (3:7). Here he makes it clear that the four giftings listed in verse 11 are not for the personal aggrandisement of those who have them, but for the benefit of everyone in the body (v.12).

But it's not only apostles and prophets and evangelists and pastor/teachers who are called to serve; everyone has a calling to 'works of service' (v.12). Whoever I am in the church I need to accept that everything I have – gifts, insights, experiences, skills – is entrusted to me so that I can offer them back to God in service to others.

8. Our calling is equally to be served by others. If we're all called to serve each other, then we must all be ready to be served by each other. If you're one of those people who find it hard to let others serve you, accept that God wants you to make a special effort in this area; for the sake of the body you need to be served just as much as you need to serve.

9. Bathe everything in love (vv.2,15–16). Paul wrote 'in love' as the final two climactic words of this whole passage on unity; 'the love of Christ' (3:18) is the key to every situation.

10. 'In all things grow up into him who is the Head, that is, Christ' (v.15).

Thank You, Lord, for the richness and variety in Your body, the Church. But thank You, too, for this difficult person, for this brother who's criticised me, for those two sisters who have fallen out with each other, for those problems over youth group policy ... Help us all to see that You've allowed them into the body so that we can all learn from them and through them grow closer to the Head.

The headship of Christ (1)
God's life, God's way

This is the third time in this letter that Paul has drawn the strongest of contrasts between Christians and non-Christians. In chapter 2 his main interest was the contrast in our status before God (2:1–10,11–22); here he's principally concerned with the way we live (v.17).

The contrast comes out strongly in two phrases: 'separated from the life of God' (v.18) and 'created to be like God' (v.24). Spend a few minutes today reflecting on each.

'Separated from the life of God.' What bleak emptiness there is in these words. We may sometimes think of those without Christ as much the same as us but simply rather less religious. But the truth is that they are 'without God in the world' (2:12), cut off from the One who is the only source of truth and goodness and beauty and life. Little wonder that, for all their pretence at respectability, they are driven by a 'continual lust' for 'every kind of impurity' (v.19), as shown by the TV programmes they choose to watch or the huge percentage of those who use the internet for porn. Without God their lives are in the stranglehold of the powers of darkness and their situation is hopeless (2:2,12).

'Created to be like God.' Not a sinner trying to be good, but a new creation, a 'new self' (v.24), the life of God Himself planted in us (v.18). Were this not so we could never be the people God wants us to be 'in true righteousness and holiness' (v.24). But because it is so, the most amazing things can happen. We no longer have to follow the corrupt desires of our old self (v.22); we have the source of a very different life in us. As we 'grow up into him who is the Head' (v.15), that life is ours to live in any situation; instead of being controlled by circumstances or by others or by our old way of behaving we can be 'new in the attitude' of our minds (v.23); we can see things differently and so act differently – God's way, not ours.

The headship of Christ (2)
Truth, anger, work

This passage touches on three very different areas of Christian living, all linked by the phrase 'for we are all members of one body' (v.25). Select the area God wants to speak to you about today, and let His Spirit show you how you can become more 'like God' (v.24) in it.

1. Truth. Maybe few of us would tell flagrant lies, but I guess we're all pretty good at bending truth to suit our own ends. Manipulating truth to put ourselves in a good light, exaggeration, promise-breaking, telling half-truths – these happen all the time in the non-Christian world, and it's hard to stop them creeping into our Christian lives. But God's standard is clear; as long as it can be spoken in love (v.15), we are to be committed to honest truth (v.25).

2. Anger. This is a natural human emotion which can be channelled constructively or destructively. We may be angry about human trafficking, and throw our energies into campaigning to have it stopped. Or we may be upset by a cutting remark from the boss and shout at the secretary. Our calling is to ensure that anger does not lead us to sin, that the devil doesn't use it to get a foothold in our minds or in the situation (vv.26–27). Grace and mercy and love and peace are all wonderful antidotes to anger, and these are all found richly in our God as we draw our life from Him.

3. Work. Few readers of *Cover to Cover Every Day* will need the command to stop supporting themselves by thieving, but verse 28 reminds us of two important facets of our daily work.

(1) It should be 'useful'; Paul's word simply means 'good'. Christians are called to look upon their daily work not primarily as a means to earn money or achieve self-worth, but as a way of serving or doing 'good' to others.

(2) What we earn isn't ours. Of course God wants us to have some money to meet our own needs, but the clear teaching here is that we earn money not just for ourselves, but so that we can give it away to help those in need.

God on the **move**

THIS FASCINATING and unusual psalm is difficult to categorise. It bears the marks of liturgical practice, almost as if it is a development of a script for a dramatic worship service. Throughout, the key 'stage directions' involve significant *movements*, with God taking the initiative and making the significant moves.

First, God *arises* (vv.1–6). The opening stanzas echo the ancient 'ark song' (cf. Num. 10) when Israel called on God to bestir Himself and – symbolised by the carrying of the ark of the covenant where the concentrated presence of God was said to reside – to lead Israel in battle against her enemies. Riding on the clouds, God brings terror to His foes but joy to His friends, fathering the orphans and freeing the prisoners (vv.5–6).

Secondly, God *advances* (vv.7–14). God marched out before His people from exodus to Sinai and through the wilderness, protecting and providing for them, conquering and settling them in the land. News of God's movements spreads like wildfire and frightens the local kings.

Finally, God *ascends* (vv.16–18). From fiery Sinai, God comes to His dwelling place on Mount Zion – a modest hill compared to the majestic mountains of Bashan but they look with envy on it because of the majesty of the God who dwells there!

Paul later playfully worked over this text (Eph. 4:7–11) showing how the Christ who has ascended in victory *gives* back the rebels He has captured (including apostles like Paul) to be His servants to the Church. Psalms like this remind us that our God is alive and active.

So we pray: Move again, Lord, march out against Your enemies, make advances into the waste places of our world, meet with the fatherless, the friendless, and the freedom-seeking; make us messengers of the good news of Your coming, mount up in majesty in our land and in our churches, melt our rebellious hearts with the realisation that 'to each one of us grace has been given as Christ apportioned it' (Eph. 4:7).

The headship of Christ (3)
Love

What a fantastic motto 'Live a life of love' (5:2) makes for a Christian. Literally Paul's words are 'Go around in love'. Some people go around in a BMW; some go around in a daze; some go around in a bad temper. We are the people who go around *in love*.

What situations are you having to face today or tomorrow? Some may look easy; some look tough. What people are impacting your life at the moment? Some you may like; some you may not. What tasks are waiting to be done? Some you welcome; others you don't. Over all of them God wants to write the word 'love'.

There are thousands of ways of showing love. Paul highlights here our words (4:29,31) and our attitudes (4:31–32). Christians who live a life of love will have no place for demeaning or abusive language that attacks or does down another. Nor will they have recourse to anger and bitterness and any sort of ill feeling. Instead they will make sure that everything they say encourages and strengthens, 'building others up' and bringing 'benefit' to those around them (4:29). And, by the power of the Holy Spirit who has marked us with His seal (4:30), and in imitation of God our Father (5:1), and of Jesus whose love paid the highest price (5:2), they will ensure that the triune God's heart is their heart, full of kindness and compassion and readiness to forgive anything (4:32).

A tall order? Yes – but our God isn't going to ask us to do something and then not give us what it takes to do it. After all, He has committed Himself to supplying all our needs according to His glorious riches in Christ Jesus (Phil. 4:19).

This is only a short passage, but it's worth reading more than once, maybe taking it very slowly and asking the Holy Spirit to show you any place in your life where you need a new infilling of love. Alternatively you could spend time bringing to mind all today's situations, relationships and events, and allowing God's Spirit to flood you with all the love you need to face them.

The headship of Christ (4) Holiness

'God's holy people' (v.3) is one of the key concepts of the Bible. 'I am the LORD who brought you up out of Egypt to be your God,' said God to His people in the wilderness, 'therefore be holy, because I am holy' (Lev. 11:45). He says the same to us (1 Pet. 1:15–16). An unholy Christian is a contradiction in terms; if we are God's people we must express His nature (v.1), and He is holy.

Beware of viewing holiness as something essentially negative, expressed in terms of what we don't do: we don't tell lies, we don't fiddle our tax returns, we don't indulge in sex outside marriage, and so on. God's holiness is gloriously positive, a burning fire of goodness and light and truth and beauty. As God's holy people we are called to radiate His goodness and light in a thousand positive ways and show the world around us the beauty of His holiness.

Nevertheless, as Paul was aware, God's people are under constant pressure to give way to unholiness, both because of the culture around us and as hangovers from our pre-Christian days (4:17–23). So here he warns us in the strongest terms against two forms of unholiness: sexual immorality and greed, with most of his emphasis on the first.

Sexual immorality. Sexual pleasure is a beautiful and holy gift from God, but like all gifts it is to be enjoyed under the headship of Christ. Always let Him be the test: how would He feel about that TV sex scene? What would be His reaction to that 'coarse joking'? Would He tune into that salacious website? Would He play around with those thoughts about so-and-so?

Greed. The essence of greed is that we set something other than God as the goal of our desire and effort. It's that that makes it idolatry (v.5). In this passage Paul may be referring to the way indulging in sexual immorality gets us hooked into an ever-increasing greed for more (4:19), but greed can take many forms, and any desire for anything that's not submitted to the headship of Christ must be rejected as out of character for the people of God.

The headship of Christ (5) Light

'God is light' (1 John 1:5). The image of the light of God blazing out into a dark world comes again and again throughout the Bible, from Genesis 1:3 to Revelation 22:5. Just as we are called to be holy because we are the people of a God who is holy, so we are called to be light because our God is light. We live under the headship of the Light of the world. These verses pick up three aspects of this.

1. Bask in the light. We don't know where the quotation in verse 14 comes from, but the most likely source is a hymn sung at baptismal services as the person being baptised came up out of the water, raised with Christ from the sleep of death (see Rom. 6:3–4). After the darkness of the night the rising sun floods the world with light; so the rising Christ floods His awakened and resurrected people with light.

'Christ will shine on you' isn't a bit of wishful thinking; it's the ardent purpose and promise of God, and unless we turn back and hide again in the darkness it must happen. The light of the holiness and love and wisdom and truth of Christ will radiate upon us and our lives. Ours is the privilege to bask in it, to let it shine on everything we are and do.

2. 'Live as children of light', or, even more bluntly, *be* light (v.8). The word Paul uses here for 'live' is the same as in verse 2: we are to 'go around' radiating the light of God. If Jesus hadn't said it, most of us would modestly reject the idea that we are the light of the world (Matt. 5:14). But He did say it. We are light, and we must shine.

3. Show up the darkness. The command to 'expose' 'the fruitless deeds of darkness' (v.11) isn't calling us to some kind of witchhunt in which we denounce others for their misdeeds. Rather it's stating that the very fact that we're radiating the light of God will itself show up the dirt and emptiness of those who follow darkness.

The headship of Christ (6)
Concentration

We've all done it. We're driving the car, and something distracts us. At the last moment we find we've drifted off course and only just manage to avoid disaster. Or someone is talking to us, but our mind is elsewhere, and we suddenly realise we can't remember a word that's been said.

To concentrate means to keep the central thing at the centre. For Christians the central thing is the lordship and headship of Christ. Six times verses 15 to 18 call us to concentrate, to be 'very careful' (literally to 'watch strictly'), not to be 'unwise', to grasp opportunities as a bargain hunter seizes the best offers at the summer sales, to avoid being thoughtless ('foolish', NIV), to 'understand' the Lord's will, and to make sure we never let our minds get fuddled by alcohol. Paul is certainly making a point!

I guess it's one we particularly need to take on board. The fact is that though, by the grace of God, we rarely deliberately choose flagrant sin, it's all too easy to drift off course in our Christian lives through lack of concentration.

We forget we're God's holy people, that we're the light of the world, that Jesus is our Lord; without realising what's happening we slip into thinking or behaving the way non-Christians do; before we know where we are we're denying the headship of Christ.

Three great secrets of concentration are given in the rest of this passage. The first is the infilling of the Holy Spirit (v.18). Keep making sure that you're filled up with Him, so that your mind and all that you are is 'filled to the measure of all the fulness of God' (3:19); that's a sure way of keeping focused on the centre. The second is each other. We need to be encouraging one another, not moaning together or talking about the weather, but helping each other to 'concentrate' by speaking together in a spirit of worship and praise (v.19).

And the third is a continual conscious act of thanksgiving to God 'always' 'for everything, in the name of our Lord Jesus Christ' (v.20).

Next Issue

Sep/Oct 2012

In September **Ian Coffey** looks at another six Minor Prophets – Micah, Habakkuk, Zephaniah, Haggai, Zechariah and Malachi. All these men lived in difficult times and spoke with clarity and courage. Their passion for God and His ways caused them to have an influence on their society, and we will think about how we might make a difference too.

In October **David Spriggs** writes on Philippians, one of Paul's best-loved letters, with its wonderful mixture of personal matters and doctrinal insight, and its dominant theme of joy. This letter contains serious challenges and insights for us today, not least to grow in our facility to live in changing circumstances with discerning love.

Also available as ebook/esubscription

Obtain your copy from CWR or a Christian bookshop.
If you would like to take out a subscription, see the order form at the back of these notes.

The headship of Christ (7)
Submission

For the next 22 verses Paul writes about human relationships. He's already written about broken barriers (2:14) and practical ways to 'live a life of love' (5:2). Now he picks up his call to humility and gentleness (4:2) by introducing the concept of submission.

Submission is out of favour today. We have rights, we're told, and we must stick up for them. But Christ didn't stick up for His rights (Phil. 2:6). Seven times in these verses God's people are called to follow His example and to 'submit' and 'obey'.

The passage starts with a general call to submission and gives as its basis 'reverence for Christ' (v.21). There are several ways we could amplify this: we revere Him by obeying His teaching (eg John 13:13–14), by following His example (John 13:15), and by making our submission to others an expression of our submission to Him (Matt. 25:40).

It's important to note that nowhere in this passage, not even in the section on masters and slaves, are we told to demand submission from others.

Husbands who've used Ephesians 5:22 to exact submission from their wives have completely misunderstood its meaning and the whole spirit of Jesus' teaching and life. Submission is never to be exacted or even expected; it's to be given freely in love and grace. Never did the Father force His Son to submit and obey; Jesus chose freely to submit to His Father's will.

The call to wives to submit to their husbands (vv.22–24) is patterned on the theme we've been following all through this letter, our submission to Christ as Head. The relationship between each bride and her husband should be as beautiful as the relationship of the bride of Christ to Him. The phrase 'in everything' (v.24) has to be understood as subject to the qualification 'in the Lord' (6:1); Paul isn't telling wives to submit to their husbands if they order them to do something sinful or if they're abusing them. But in everything that is 'in the Lord' Christian wives are called to express freely their submission to the headship of Christ by submission to their husbands.

Keeping **pace** with **God**

WHAT CHARACTERISES this psalm, as we noted, are the *movements* described – and, particularly, the moves God makes which bring Him to Jerusalem (v.18c). Now, in the second half of the psalm, the ancient directions for the drama of worship spell out *the moves and speeches made by the worshippers.*

Now that God has 'moved in' to the Temple, as it were, all the responses made in worship are orientated to His dwelling place there and all the moves are made in its direction (enemies brought there, v.22; worshippers entering there, v.24; tribute brought there, v.29).

The psalm first pictures God's people *blessing* Him for daily bearing their burdens and saving them from premature death (vv.19–20); then *processing* into the sanctuary (vv.24–27) as if in ritualised reenactment of God's own victory march. The procession is led by singers backed by musicians (a hint for contemporary worship groups?) and spearheaded by the least of the tribal clans (vv.25,27) as the whole congregation gathers to praise the Lord (v.26) and pray for His rule to be recognised on a wider scale (vv.29–31). Thirdly, the assembled worshippers are seen *addressing* the wider world (vv.32–35) as worship overspills into witness to the universal attractiveness of our God. So this intriguing psalm invites us still to *praise the Lord, to join His procession, to engage in intercession, and to accept our mission of telling the world how great God is.*

We celebrate a God of majesty who rides high in triumph over His enemies (vv.4,33) but does not ride roughshod over the needy (vv.5–6). The dynamo of love that energises God's every move is the 'power and strength' He gave to Israel (v.35) and now, by His Spirit, given to us to enable us to perform 'the good works which God has prepared in advance for us to do' (Eph. 2:10). When God is on the move, it's all we can do to keep up with Him. But by the divine power at work within us, we will, and He will get the glory (Eph. 3:20–21).

The headship of Christ (8) Husbands and wives

I guess you, like me, have come across all sorts of Christian marriages. There are those that are radiantly beautiful; there are those where things have turned sour; and there are plenty somewhere in between.

How do we ensure that a marriage is radiantly beautiful? In addition to all that we've learnt so far in this letter about love and holiness and light, this passage gives us four key principles. Use them to do a check-up on your own marriage relationship, or as fuel for prayer and pastoral care of couples with whom you're involved.

1. Ensure that everything about the marriage is under the headship of Christ (v.30). Every couple needs continually to make Christ the head of their relationship and all that they do.

2. Love as Christ loved (v.25). That's the standard, nothing less than the love of Jesus, and it sets in context all the debates over 'submission' and the like. When both partners in a marriage truly 'live a life of love' (v.2) every element of their relationship, including submission and headship, will be wholesome and beautiful.

3. Give yourself up (v.25). Christ has done it for us; we must do it for each other. The challenge to Christian husbands, that they should love their wives to the extent of being willing to die for them, is in a sense even more costly than the call to wives to submit to their husbands. It reflects the true meaning of agape love which is empty of anything self-centred, and will stop short of nothing for the wellbeing of the one who is loved.

4. Value each other very highly. However much non-Christians may belittle or make digs about their partners, we are called to 'honour' (the word means 'value' or even 'prize') 'one another above' ourselves (Rom. 12:10). It is this that underlies the readiness to 'submit' (v.22) and 'respect' (v.33); it also lies behind the picture in verse 27 of a husband fired with the vision of empowering his wife to become 'radiant', 'without stain or wrinkle or any other blemish, but holy and blameless'.

The headship of Christ (9) Parents and children

We'll concentrate today on the responsibilities of parents (v.4). Negatively, we're to avoid exasperating (literally 'provoking to anger') our children; positively, we're to provide them with training and instruction in Jesus. Parenting is a hugely complex task; parents need all the help and wisdom they can get, and there are few simple answers to the many issues they may face. But here are four principles that arise from this verse.

1. Show children respect. Affirm them. Show how much you love and value them. One of the chief sources of 'exasperation' is a sense of being ignored or rejected or misunderstood. Remember at all stages to accept them as they are: don't blame a child for being childish, and equally never criticise an adolescent for behaving like an adolescent. Accept them even if you don't like or don't understand where they're at. Always make time to listen to them; make it a principle that your children will spend more time talking with you than glued to a computer or TV screen.

2. Give them secure structures ('training'). Children need to learn from their parents what is right and what is wrong, good and bad. Later in life they'll have the freedom to decide whether or not to hold on to the structures they've been given, but to leave everything open from the start will lead not just to insecurity but to chaos. Explain to them why you impose principles and boundaries; give them opportunities to question and even challenge them. Seek as far as you can to be consistent without being rigid; let love and grace govern everything, and be willing if necessary to admit you've got things wrong.

3. Teach them God's truth. Too many Christian parents leave 'instruction of the Lord' to the youth workers at the church. The Bible puts the responsibility squarely on the parents (Deut. 6:6-7).

4. Surround them with Jesus. Whatever 'training and instruction' we give, it must be 'of the Lord'. Our primary responsibility to our children is to show them Jesus, through who we are, what we do, and what we say.

The headship of Christ (10) Slaves and masters

Not many of us are masters and even fewer are slaves. But there's vital teaching here that has a much wider application than just the first-century slavery system.

Christian slaves, assumes Paul, should be the best slaves of all. They should serve well, work hard, and show due respect to their masters and mistresses (vv.5–7). Of course, slavery in itself was a bad thing, full of all sorts of evils. But that didn't change the fact that Christian slaves should be the best slaves of all.

In the same way Christian employees or voluntary workers should be the best workers. Granted, the boss may be a bad boss, or the system may be useless, but that doesn't change the fact that Christian workers should be the best workers. What's more, Christian drivers should be the best drivers on the road. Granted, some of the speed limits or rules of the road may seem to be unnecessary, but that doesn't alter the fact that Christian drivers should be exemplary road users.

Again, Christian neighbours should be the best neighbours. And plumbers (however unreliable) should know that if they're called to a Christian house they'll be treated as though it is Jesus who's got the blocked drain. Shop assistants and check-out workers should be delighted when they get a Christian customer, knowing they'll be shown respect and friendliness. And so on.

There are all sorts of reasons for this. It's vital, of course, for our witness; we can be sure we're always being watched, not just by those around us but by our Master in heaven (v.9). And then there's the issue of rewards (v.8). But the main reason is that whatever we do we do for Jesus (v.7): 'It is the Lord Christ you are serving' (Col. 3:24).

So we come to the end of this long section on the practical implications of living here and now under the headship of Christ. One day, in the fulness of God's great purposes, everything will be under the headship of Christ (1:10). Ours is the privilege of experiencing and showing to the world a foretaste of His amazing plan.

Into battle together under the headship of Christ

I guess all of us have been greatly helped by this marvellous passage as we've personally put on the armour of God and taken our stand in the battle against the powers of evil. Indeed, you may feel that that is the most appropriate way to apply it as you read it through today.

However, there's another way of applying it, and that's to the whole Church, especially the local community of God's people. As we've seen, our oneness together under the headship of Christ is a central theme of the letter, so it must be legitimate, as we come to the letter's end, to apply its final teaching in that context.

In ancient warfare victory was generally won not by lots of individual soldiers fighting their separate battles but by a solid 'phalanx' of soldiers standing together as one. This passage isn't just a call to individuals to be equipped with God's armour in the fight against the powers of evil; it's a vision of a local church, armed and equipped, 'contending as one man' (Phil. 1:27), 'strong' together 'in the Lord' (v.10), standing together 'against the devil's schemes' (v.11), and winning victories together over the 'powers of this dark world' (v.12).

To do this, God's people need to stand firm together in the truth and live out consistently the righteousness of God (v.14); we all need to be trained to share the good news with those around us (v.15), and to stand firm together in faith and the knowledge that we are truly the redeemed people of God (vv.16–17). In every battle we must together depend wholly on the Word of God (v.17). Above all we must be encouraging one another and keeping one another 'alert' as we pray together on every occasion and in every way (v.18).

An individual equipped with the armour of God will see great things achieved in the battle against evil. How much more will be achieved when a whole church together is equipped with this armour, and, in love and unity, under the headship and lordship of Christ and in His 'mighty power', fulfils God's great purpose for it in the world.

Final call

For the fifth time in this letter Paul writes of the 'mystery' of the gospel (v.19), that great purpose of God once unknown, but now revealed to us His people, summed up in 1:10 as 'to bring all things in heaven and on earth together under one head, even Christ'.

If you pray for me at all, he says, pray not so much for an easy life, or safety in travel, or release from prison. Rather, pray that 'whenever I open my mouth, words may be given me so that I will fearlessly make known the mystery of the gospel' (v.19). Then he repeats it, 'Pray that I may declare it fearlessly' (v.20). He knew what he'd get: mockery, rejection, persecution, floggings, imprisonment, martyrdom – enough to make anyone scared. So pray, he says, that even if I am scared and tempted to stay silent, I'll still do what God has called me to do – declare the mystery of the gospel.

That's the final call of God to us as we come to the end of this letter. God is working out His amazing purpose, to bring to an end the rebellion and fragmentation of this world. We are part of that purpose; already we know reconciliation with God and with each other and the glory of living under the headship of Christ. But many still aren't aware of this purpose. So God's call to us, however much it costs, is to make it a priority that they should know it, both as a revealed truth and in practice as they see it working out in our lives, so that, by God's grace, they'll come to experience it for themselves.

How many times have you prayed 'Your kingdom come'? There's no doubt that it will come 'when the times will have reached their fulfilment' (1:10). But meanwhile God's purpose is that it should be coming in and through and around His people as together we fulfil our calling to be 'faithful servants in the Lord' (v.21) and to live under His headship lives filled with peace and love and faith and grace (vv.23–24) – lives filled with Jesus.

ORDER FORM

5 EASY WAYS TO ORDER:

1. Phone in your credit card order: **01252 784710** (Mon–Fri, 9.30am – 5pm)
2. Visit our Online Store at **www.cwr.org.uk/store**
3. Send this form together with your payment to:
   CWR, Waverley Abbey House, Waverley Lane, Farnham, Surrey GU9 8EP
4. Visit your local Christian bookshop
5. For Australia and New Zealand visit KI Entertainment at **www.cwr4u.net.au**

For a list of our National Distributors, who supply countries outside the UK, visit www.cwr.org.uk/distributors

YOUR DETAILS (REQUIRED FOR ORDERS AND DONATIONS)

Name:	**CWR ID No.** (if known):
Home Address:	
	Postcode:
Telephone No. (for queries):	**Email:**

PUBLICATIONS

TITLE	QTY	PRICE	TOTAL
		Total publications	

All CWR adult Bible-reading notes are also available in ebook and email subscription format.
Visit www.cwr.org.uk for further information.

UK p&p: up to £24.99 = **£2.99**; £25.00 and over = **FREE**

Elsewhere p&p: up to £10 = **£4.95**; £10.01 - £50 = **£6.95**; £50.01 - £99.99 = **£10**; £100 and over = **£30**

Please allow 14 days for delivery	Total publications and p&p **A**	

SUBSCRIPTIONS* (NON DIRECT DEBIT)	QTY	PRICE (INCLUDING P&P)			TOTAL
		UK	Europe	Elsewhere	
Every Day with Jesus (1yr, 6 issues)		£15.50	£19.25	Please contact nearest National Distributor or CWR direct	
Large Print *Every Day with Jesus* (1yr, 6 issues)		£15.50	£19.25		
Inspiring Women Every Day (1yr, 6 issues)		£15.50	£19.25		
Life Every Day (Jeff Lucas) (1yr, 6 issues)		£15.50	£19.25		
Cover to Cover Every Day (1yr, 6 issues)		£15.50	£19.25		
Mettle: 14–18s (1yr, 3 issues)		£13.80	£15.90		
YP's: 11–15s (1yr, 6 issues)		£15.50	£19.25		
Topz: 7–11s (1yr, 6 issues)		£15.50	£19.25		
Total Subscriptions (Subscription prices already include postage and packing) **B**					

Please circle which bimonthly issue you would like your subscription to commence from:

JAN/FEB MAR/APR MAY/JUN JUL/AUG SEP/OCT NOV/DEC

* Only use this section for subscriptions paid for by credit/debit card or
cheque. For Direct Debit subscriptions see overleaf.

CONTINUED OVERLEAF >>

‹‹ SEE PREVIOUS PAGE FOR START OF ORDER FORM

PAYMENT DETAILS

☐ I enclose a cheque/PO made payable to CWR for the amount of: **£**

☐ Please charge my credit/debit card.

Cardholder's name (in BLOCK CAPITALS)

Card No. ☐☐☐☐ ☐☐☐☐ ☐☐☐☐ ☐☐☐☐

Expires end ☐☐ ☐☐   Security Code ☐☐☐

GENERAL DONATION TO CWR   ☐ Please send me an acknowledgement of my gift   **C** ☐

GIFT AID (YOUR HOME ADDRESS REQUIRED, SEE OVERLEAF)

giftaid it

I am a UK taxpayer and want CWR to reclaim the tax on all my donations for the four years prior to this year **and on** all donations I make from the date of this Gift Aid declaration until further notice.*

Taxpayer's Full Name (in BLOCK CAPITALS)

Signature _____ **Date** _____

*I understand I must pay an amount of Income/Capital Gains Tax at least equal to the tax the charity reclaims in the tax year.

GRAND TOTAL (Total of A, B & C) ☐

SUBSCRIPTIONS BY DIRECT DEBIT (UK BANK ACCOUNT HOLDERS ONLY)

Subscriptions cost £15.50 (except *Mettle*: £13.80) for one year for delivery within the UK. Please tick relevant boxes and fill in the form bel

☐ *Every Day with Jesus* (1yr, 6 issues)
☐ Large Print *Every Day with Jesus* (1yr, 6 issues)
☐ *Inspiring Women Every Day* (1yr, 6 issues)
☐ *Life Every Day* (Jeff Lucas) (1yr, 6 issues)

☐ *Cover to Cover Every Day* (1yr, 6 issues)
☐ *Mettle:* 14-18s (1yr, 3 issues)
☐ *YP's:* 11-15s (1yr, 6 issues)
☐ *Topz:* 7-11s (1yr, 6 issues)

Issue to commence from:
☐ Jan/Feb ☐ Jul/Aug
☐ Mar/Apr ☐ Sep/Oct
☐ May/Jun ☐ Nov/Dec

CWR   Instruction to your Bank or Building Society to pay by Direct Debit   **DIRECT Debit**

Please fill in the form and send to: CWR, Waverley Abbey House, Waverley Lane, Farnham, Surrey GU9 8EP

Name and full postal address of your Bank or Building Society

To: The Manager   Bank/Building Society
Address
Postcode

Name(s) of Account Holder(s)

Branch Sort Code ☐☐ ☐☐ ☐☐

Bank/Building Society account number ☐☐☐☐☐☐☐☐

Originator's Identification Number 4 2 0 4 8 7

Reference ☐☐☐☐☐☐☐☐☐☐☐☐☐☐☐☐☐☐

Instruction to your Bank or Building Society
Please pay CWR Direct Debits from the account detailed in this Instruction subject to the safeguards assured by the Direct Debit Guarantee.
I understand that this Instruction may remain with CWR and, if so, details will be passed electronically to my Bank/Building Society.

Signature(s)

Date

Banks and Building Societies may not accept Direct Debit Instructions for some types of account